The **TITLE I** Teacher's Guide to Teaching *Reading*

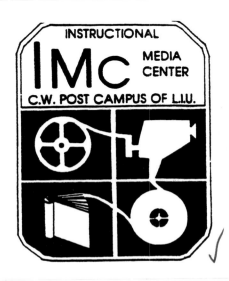

K–3

The TITLE I Teacher's Guide to Teaching *Reading*

Nancy Akhavan

HEINEMANN
Portsmouth, NH

Heinemann
A division of Reed Elsevier Inc.
361 Hanover Street
Portsmouth, NH 03801–3912
www.heinemann.com

Offices and agents throughout the world

© 2008 by Nancy Akhavan

The author and publisher wish to thank those who have generously given permission to reprint borrowed material:

Cover image and excerpt from *Baby Bear's Present* by Beverly Randell. Copyright © 1994. Published by Rigby. Reprinted with permission from Thomson Learning Australia.

Cover image from *Lizard Loses His Tail* by Beverly Randell. Copyright © 2000. Published by Rigby. Reprinted with permission from Thomson Learning Australia.

Library of Congress Cataloging-in-Publication Data
Akhavan, Nancy L.
  The Title I teacher's guide to teaching reading, K–3 / Nancy Akhavan ; foreword by Denise Rea.
       p. cm.
  Includes bibliographical references and index.
  ISBN-13: 978-0-325-01083-0
  ISBN-10: 0-325-01083-8
  1. Reading (Elementary)—United States. 2. Reading—Remedial teaching—United States. 3. Reading comprehension—Study and teaching (Elementary)—United States. 4. Children with social disabilities—Education—United States. 5. Federal aid to education—United States. I. Title. II. Title: Title 1 teacher's guide to teaching reading, K–3. III. Title: Title One teacher's guide to teaching reading, K–3.
LB1573.A37 2007
372.41—dc22   2007023717

Editor: Lisa Luedeke
Production: Lynne Costa
Cover design: Shawn Girsberger
Typesetter: Publishers' Design and Production Services, Inc.
Manufacturing: Louise Richardson

Printed in the United States of America on acid-free paper

12 11 10 09 08   VP   1 2 3 4 5

To Hollie, Pam, and Kristina,
for simply everything

Contents

Foreword

"Reading and writing workshops won't work in this era of testing and accountability."

"I need to teach the skills so that my students will score well on the district tests they have to take."

"My principal wants to see that I'm teaching the reading and writing skills that students need to be able to become readers, and that means I have to use the district-adopted text, not trade books."

I often hear comments like these in schools. Teachers won't even try to implement reading workshops, because they're afraid their students won't learn the skills that will be tested, or because their principals won't approve.

Here's a principal who does approve. In *The Title I Teacher's Guide to Teaching Reading*, Nancy Akhavan shows primary teachers why workshops are good for students, even those who struggle, and especially those who are English language learners. Drawing on her experiences as a principal, a reading staff developer, and a teacher, she shows us how teachers use reading and writing workshops successfully.

In Nancy's Title I school, where many students are English language learners living in a diverse community entrenched in poverty, effective teaching is critical. These students can be difficult to teach because they come to school speaking a language other than English and have different background experiences and gaps in their understanding. Many also come with a history of failure. These students need help to catch up with their more privileged peers.

In this book Nancy shows teachers exactly what constitutes an effective workshop: how long each part of the workshop lasts, what the students do, what the teacher says and does. She also shares the blank templates, or frames, she uses to support struggling students and to organize their thinking for writing. She includes samples of student work so that teachers can immediately implement the workshops and see whether they are on track by comparing these samples with their own students' work. Nancy takes the guesswork out of teaching literacy using workshops and makes it easy to get started.

Several critical ideas are emphasized here. The first is the need to be *purposeful*. I love the idea of being purposeful in your teaching. Being purposeful means there is no time to waste, that every move the teacher makes has a purpose—a purpose that engenders student learning. It means being explicit about instruction and student learning outcomes in relation to the grade-level standards. Nancy's literacy program improves student learning because it teaches students how to

- explicitly construct knowledge
- participate in purposeful activities
- make meaning while immersed in language.

Another assertion Nancy makes is that the work *students* do in a workshop must also be purposeful or intentional. Teachers can't *tell* children how to read, they have to show them. And showing means directing, modeling, coaching, and guiding. There is no room for mindless activities or "stuff," no room for "worksheet-driven activities like coloring, tracing, crafts, and fill-in-the-blank tasks." These are not the activities that nurture reading.

In Nancy's workshop, students record their thoughts after they read. The process of thinking and writing about their thinking "deepens their comprehension of the book and gives them practice with reading and writing strategies." Reading and writing are the work children need to do each day, and this is what happens in the well-designed and well-implemented workshops that Nancy creates.

Teachers who value rich literacy instruction understand that reading and writing matter so much that they must find time for these subjects every day. And every day they will provide some kind of intentional instruction about the practices of reading and writing—not just assign pages to read or papers to write. This book encourages and inspires. It is a helpful resource for primary teachers in their efforts to design and carry out their own workshops.

Denise Rea
Director of Multiple Subjects
Fresno Pacific University

Acknowledgments

In 2004 I was lucky enough to become the principal of a vibrant school in central California that was struggling to meet No Child Left Behind mandates. Pinedale Elementary School is located in an urban neighborhood where many children receive a free or reduced-price lunch. The staff members there were energetic and dedicated but unsure why the test scores of the spring high-stakes exam were sliding down instead of going up. They were working very, very hard but not seeing the results they had hoped for.

The team embarked on creating a literacy model that implemented best practices in literacy instruction while watching state standards and focusing on effective assessment to keep tabs on children's daily progress. The model the teachers and I created together worked. Test scores rose, and children were involved in purposeful literacy work each and every day.

This book is the outcome of the work of all the people who came together to create the magic of this enterprise. Specifically I want to thank all of the primary teachers who taught at Pinedale Elementary School during these formidable years: Lori Garcia-Higgs, Anissa Medina, Christine Aguirre, Kristina Karlson, Aide Madrigal, Robin Prigmore, Thea Tan, Michele Hart, Laurie Cruz, Hollie Olsen, Pamela Pflepsen, Gloria Tovar, Patti Moore, Susie Parker, Kent Sherwood, Laurel Graves, Bethany Marinovich, Shelley Vizcarra, Kathy Nation, and Dava Parks. This book exists because of their openness and their desire to improve instruction and share their learning with many people.

I would be remiss if I didn't thank the team behind the scenes at the district office who supported the work that allowed the school to flourish. Their support was invaluable. Terry Bradley, Dan Kaiser, Ginny Boris, Lyn Snauffer, Rosalie Baker, and Debbie Parra never wavered in their belief that this literacy model would work for our children. Many others came together and participated in our professional learning community. I thank the hundreds of principals and teachers who have visited the school; while there are too many people to name individually, their questions and desire to understand guided my writing so that I could be clear and focused.

I also want to thank the Heinemann team who helped this project become a book and continue to support my growth as a writer and an educator. I have been blessed to work with Lynne Costa for more than four years. Each time one of my manuscripts arrives on her desk, she works with such care to produce a beautiful book. Thanks also to Lisa Luedeke for her careful editing but most of all for coming to the school so that together we could envision the best way to facilitate the learning of all readers. I continue to be blessed by many others at Heinemann, including Leigh Peake, Maura Sullivan, Alan Huisman, Angela Dion, and Stephanie Colado. Thank you for your dedication to great educational models.

My children, Sayeh and Naseem, have now adjusted to the fact that I teach, write, and work, and in between I am home. I love them for their patience but also for their prodding me to write another book. To my husband, Mehran, thank you for always being with me for the ride on the roller coaster of school reform. I couldn't do this arduous work without you.

Introduction

I could begin by telling you that if you follow a scripted literacy program to meet the needs of your at-risk students, your life will be easier. I could tell you that if you do so your students will meet accountability measures and they will read and write well by the end of the school year, hands down. I could say, "Just follow the program, and you will get results." I could tell you that I have seen wonderful results when teachers followed the lesson plans in the teachers' guides; that teaching isn't rocket science; that you, alone, can meet the needs of all your students with the perfect program.

I could tell you these things, but I am not going to.

While many people adhere to the idea that there is a magic formula for solving the literacy ills we face in the classroom and beyond, scripted programs aren't the only way to achieve success in your classroom. There are other ways. But it is important to realize there exists no perfect program to raise student achievement. Truly successful schools and teachers focus on learning, but the learning they focus on might surprise you: they focus on their own learning first.

The best way to ensure student achievement is to start with the teacher. In order for students to learn, teachers first have to learn about the students and tailor their instruction to meet the students' needs. This means you have to reflect on your current practices as well as research and implement purposeful and effective reading and writing strategies in order to improve your instruction. The National Reading Panel report points out that those teachers who educate themselves on effective teaching strategies give themselves control over instructional decision making that can, in turn, affect student learning (NICHD 2000).

And perhaps if we focus on our learning, we won't need a scripted program at all. Maybe what we really need is to develop an understanding of how the reading process works and to figure out how children who often struggle in school can in fact learn to read and write.

Research tells us that the achievement gap between minority students and white students persists despite efforts and policies focused on equal opportunities to learn for all students. The American Educational Research Association (2004a) states, "By 12th grade, the average African American and Hispanic student can only do math and read as well as a white eighth grader. In addition, high school completion rates remain markedly lower for students of color" (1). *What* children are taught and *how* children are taught in the primary grades pave the way for the learning they will do in the upper-elementary grades, before they even embark on their secondary education. The skills, strategies, and knowledge they acquire in our primary classrooms are essential. We build the foundation upon which their future education rests.

Just because you work in a school that serves a high proportion of children of color or children living in poverty doesn't mean your students can't learn things that students in other schools do. But in order for them to learn, *you* have to begin with knowing.

- Know your literacy program goals.
- Know your literacy program structures and routines.
- Know your students.
- Know that they will achieve if you create the environment and experiences that nurture and assume success.

But just knowing is not enough. You also have to implement and apply what you know. There is a persistent gap between what we know we need to do and what we actually do when it comes to instruction (Pfeffer and Sutton 2000). This gap is common. Research reveals through classroom observations that effective literacy practices are not always implemented. In fact the results of fifteen hundred classroom observations reveal the following (Reeves 2006):

- A clear objective was present only 4 percent of the time.
- Worksheets were used in 52 percent of the lessons observed.
- Lecture was used instead of short, precise lessons 32 percent of the time
- Monitoring with no feedback was used in 22 percent of the lessons.

Teaching in a Title I School

Each school year brings the promise of new beginnings. I approached this book project much like I approach my building each year in August—I am full of hope and wonder and my notebook is full of ideas. At the beginning of this year I came to school a couple of weeks after summer school ended and stepped into a silent, solitary office. Scattered upon my desk were the remnants of projects I had launched during the summer. A rolled-up piece of butcher paper lay in one corner; outlined on it was the professional development plan for the new school year. On the corner of my desk were stacks of student writing from last spring. A few wayward papers stuck out from the stack. When I glanced at them, I saw words in big, first-grade, scrawling print. On the other side of my desk sat paper and binders outlining the district plan. Mixed into the mess was a wad of sticky notes filled with hieroglyphics from classroom visits I had made in the spring. As I scanned my desk, the scattering of papers and notes reminded me of my goal: help teachers guide children to learn.

At my school this isn't easy. My staff and I serve children who receive free and reduced-price lunches, who speak English as a second language, and who battle the challenges of an urban neighborhood. My school, located in the San Joaquin valley of California, is designated a Title I school. As a Title I school, we receive federal funding to raise student achievement. We also face the scrutiny of high-stakes testing and public reporting programs.

During my years in education, success has never come easy for my students. I have always taught the children who need an extra boost to make school meaningful. Many have parents who work long, hard days in the service industry or as farmworkers or in other labor-intensive jobs. Some come from homes caught in a cycle of poverty; their parents are incarcerated and they are cared for by various relatives or friends. Some of the children help raise younger siblings while their parents toil. Other children come from homes that have a less than positive view of school; perhaps school was not a good experience for their parents. I've also worked with children whose parents put education high on the list but didn't know how to approach the school with concerns and needs. I've seen children face prejudice in their neighborhoods and beyond. I have met some educators who would rather not teach in my school, and I have worked with others who would never dream of leaving.

Throughout the years that have I worked in Title I schools, both federal and state mandates have governed some of our decisions, laying parameters to judge our success as teachers, but never has the pressure been as high as it is with current legislative accountability. I've attended numerous compliance meetings, assessment rollouts, and program inservices, all of which were designed to solve the difficulties I faced in my classroom. From these experiences, I have gained a perspective and an understanding: when we learn to teach better, we can help children learn in powerful ways. It is possible to overcome the odds and teach children not only to learn but also to love learning and view school as purposeful in their lives.

The children served in the schools I have worked with are often performing below grade level. They are often struggling readers and writers, but not always. It is hard to define this type of child without creating an inappropriate label. So, in this text I refer to the children who often score below expectations on state standardized tests, on reading assessments, and on our writing rubrics as *the children who need support*. These students are successful when a combination of many factors is present, but most often it is because they have a focused teacher who scaffolds their learning and clearly targets state curriculum expectations. However, there is more to it than that: the teacher must have a firm belief that her students can achieve more than the bare minimum. We need to reach *beyond* the compliance guidelines and mandates. We have to teach as if the children can learn anything. All we have to do is create a literacy-rich environment, teach effective lessons, and then let them go. It really does work.

In the remainder of this book, I will show you how.

CHAPTER ONE

Moving Beyond Compliance
Effective Literacy Instruction for All Children

The children are spread out on the floor across the room. In fact, when I swing open the classroom door, I have to lift my foot in order not to disturb the child in front of me. Jenny sits on her heels, her back toward the door. She is carefully laying the books from her book box on the floor in front of her. She picks each one up, lovingly runs her hand across the cover, and sets it down, forming a semicircle of learning around her. I linger behind Jenny for a moment, long enough to see her choose one of the books and begin reading, a pad of sticky notes beside her, ready for note taking. I glance up and see the other children in the room fanned out into every nook and cranny. They are settling in as well, each with her or his own goal and style. Jorgé pulls the books from his box quickly; the books tumble out and land on his leg, along with a wad of crumpled paper and some pencil shavings. Catherine is walking around, book box in hand, her black pony-tails with pink barrettes bobbing with each step; she is searching for the perfect place to settle in.

There is different air in this room; I inhale and a pleasant fragrance fills my lungs. It smells like vanilla but feels like books. Different sounds spring up. Children to my right giggle over a picture in a book; across the room a quiet murmur begins as the children read their books aloud to themselves. First-grade rooms tend not to be quiet places, even during independent reading, but this room is alive; it is full of readers.

"Oh, hi," Kristina calls from across the room as she waves me over. I gingerly step over Jenny and head over to Kristina. "I just started a new unit of study, and I'm not sure I did it right."

"What do you mean, 'did it right'?" I ask.

"Well, they are spending time reading their just-right books, and then they are going to do some research in their nonfiction books. I showed them how to take notes today and how nonfiction can really excite our senses. I am just worried that it is too much and they won't be able to take the notes and think about their reading."

"Well," I say, surveying the room again, "from the looks of things, you're off to a great start!"

"I'm still worried." Kristina stops for a moment and redirects one child who is having trouble getting started.

"Don't worry," I say. "If you mess up the lesson, the kids won't care. They will follow your lead."

Following the Lead

Following the lead isn't always easy. Sometimes, just sometimes, we doubt ourselves more than we should. Sometimes when I can't find the lead, it is right there in front of me, in the children who come to school every day. I just have to be brave enough to reach out and snatch it. When I do, I am rewarded. By following their lead, I am able to teach minilessons with purpose and potential for learning; I am able to assess student learning and look to the next day's lesson to ensure student success. But it isn't always this way.

Many days I lose the lead or am afraid to snatch it up. Sometimes late at night, I worry: Will the kids learn to read well enough so we will meet district expectations? Will we teach all the standards we are expected to teach? Will the children learn? Will they succeed? Will I fail? And then, as the night thickens and the lights on my clock radio slowly burn through the numbers in the dark, my mind turns to everything I haven't done for the readers and writers in my school; I lose my lead. Those nights are especially frequent when state tests are looming or after a newspaper's headlines blare recent sanctions on a "low-performing" school. In the morning, I get myself to work quickly and greet the children. Seeing them each day, I feel reconnected. When they tell me their needs and wishes or share what they had for dinner the night before or how angry they were at their sisters and brothers for some misdeed, I find my lead again: it is the children.

I teach and work in a challenging school, so I focus on the children. To succeed in teaching linguistically and culturally diverse students, children of color, and children of poverty, I have to focus on what I *can* accomplish, not what I may *not* be able to accomplish. Find your lead, and take the children from their current academic standing to wherever you want to them go. Be a dreamer, and then a realist; be a master teacher, and a mom or dad; be an educator who is out to make a difference, and begin with the children in your class lineup this morning. If you mess up, don't worry. The kids won't care; they will just be eager for their next literacy adventure. What is important is that you reflect on the problem, adjust, and keep going.

A Vision of Cohesive Literacy Instruction: Units of Study

Your literacy program will roll out in a cohesive and connected manner if you organize your reading workshop through units of study. When you create a scope and sequence for your instruction based on grade-level expectations, standards, and student needs, you not only ensure learning but protect this valuable and connected teaching time. It is easier for your administrator to support reading workshop when you know what you are going to accomplish during a given school year and then provide artifacts of student learning (book lists, responses to literature pieces, running records, other assessment results) that show how much your students learned. It is equally powerful to take the qualitative data you collect at the end of the year, reflect on how they relate to your overall workshop goals, and revise your plans.

There is a caveat though! To move beyond compliance and to create a classroom designed to support students who come to school without the same literacy experiences as children from higher socioeconomic backgrounds, your unit of study plans must go beyond what a textbook, or basal program, says should occur in your classroom. Sometimes you also have to move beyond standards if you find them limiting. Some standards actually don't expect enough of students. Standards that are designed as lists and lists of items students are supposed to know but that do not show *how* the students should know the information may actually limit students' learning by overcompartmentalizing expectations. Your workshops need to be based on goals that guide reading and writing with depth and breadth and encourage students to construct knowledge and apply it to purposeful experiences. The effective classroom is a balance between purposeful, integrated opportunities to practice learning and precise, direct instruction.

Over the nineteen years that I have worked with schools serving children of color and poverty, I have seen hundreds of classrooms. In many, I find the same thing missing. Often, because of the daily struggle of meeting the children's academic, emotional, and physical needs, the schools or the classrooms lack a unifying cohesiveness. The curriculum, goals, atmosphere, and materials are not connected. Sometimes this occurs in classrooms where the teachers doubt themselves too much. In the wake of their desire to improve, they have latched onto programs, hoping that one of them will work. These rooms are filled with a bit of this and a bit of that from a multitude of programs or teaching ideas. By unifying your program around transactional instruction, you can choose what works best in your units of study and coordinate your daily schedule, materials, curriculum, and goals (Pressley and Harris 2006). When the classroom literacy program is focused on making meaning and ensuring that children have the skills to access the text, children learn (Cambourne 2002; Taylor 2002).

Assessment

Successful schools have a plethora of connected, focused classrooms (Taylor, Peterson, et al. 2002: Taylor, Pressley, and Pearson 2002). The teachers find their lead and stay focused on what they want to accomplish. As I mentioned, sometimes it is hard to find the lead, especially if you are attempting to move beyond the scope and sequence laid out for you in a textbook and create a meaningful sequence of instruction through cohesive units of study. Assessment is key to finding your lead.

Assess Yourself and Your Classroom

To develop a focused and purposeful literacy program in your classroom, you first need to assess where you are as a teacher. What do you have in place to support learning? Do you have any of the following in place?

- reading workshop approach
- library filled with books and print from many genres
- book partner schedule to support student reading and response
- small-group meeting area for focused teaching
- book boxes to hold independent and instructional texts
- response journals to guide comprehension development
- colorful and engaging walls that focus on teaching and that help create a literacy-rich environment
- appropriate assessments to monitor student progress in multiple ways

Assess Your Understanding of State Standards

You also need to be well versed in the multiple ways standards guide your curriculum. Work with grade-level teams and assess your understanding of your state standards. Do you know what they look like as performances in the classroom? Effective standards go beyond checklists and focus on what the children should be able to do. Do you need to examine national standards in order to understand how the state standards can be coordinated and described as a student performance? Any unit of study you create must be based on your students' needs, but the standards can lead you where you are going. For example, a performance standard might state, *by the end of first grade, a student will read with fluency and accuracy from an unseen text that has been previewed for them at level I*; this criteria is based on the Primary Literacy Standards by the National Center on Education and the Economy (NCEE 2001).

So the purpose of assessment is twofold: to understand student ability and learning needs and to understand how students apply their learning to standards-based performances.

Kidwatching to Assess Students' Abilities and Learning Needs

I continually assess the students I work with. I watch to see whether they are interacting with text, talking to partners, actively listening, writing, focusing on meaning, reading, decoding, comprehending, and enjoying. I incorporate a kidwatching stance into my daily interactions. Some of my assessment is instantaneous. I watch, listen, take notes, and develop understanding. While kidwatching, you begin to understand the role of errors or mistakes in reading and language learning. Errors, additions, and miscues reveal the child's current ability level. In essence, by carefully watching children, you can understand how concepts currently exist in the child's schema (Owocki and Goodman 2002). By knowing the degree of the children's conceptual development, you will know how and what to teach in order to help them meet grade-level expectations and more.

Once you incorporate a kidwatching stance into your day, you will collect large amounts of information about your students. To help monitor their progress, keep samples of their work in a portfolio or assessment folder as examples of their learning. When you take time to compare samples against a rubric or guiding document to evaluate student performance, you can identify learning gaps and plan instruction accordingly. Your formative assessments should validate your anecdotal notes and your understanding of student development. When you truly understand your students' reading and writing abilities, there will be few surprises in the spring when state testing comes around.

Select assessments that meet the expectations of your district and complement your cohesive, meaning-centered program. If you give, or are expected to give, standards-based, bubble-in-type tests, make sure you are following up with "in-touch" assessments, like kidwatching, taking anecdotal notes, examining student writing with a rubric, and taking a running record. These kinds of assessments will give you a clearer picture of student needs and will help you plan instruction (Owocki and Goodman 2002). They keep you in touch with your students' ability and reveal what your next teaching step should be. To move beyond compliance to meaning-connected results, you have to leave assign-and-assess teaching to one side. You have to get involved with your students and with the curriculum. Yes, in the beginning it is hard, but it is also extremely rewarding. Soon, the effort it takes to teach a workshop, plan, and assess will lessen. This kind of teaching will become part of your new routine and will take much less time and energy as time goes on.

Teaching with Rigor

Teach with rigor. This is a theme I have revisited many times with colleagues and teachers in my workshops. But what does *rigor* mean? When I say *teach with rigor*, I am not referring to assign-and-assess instruction. I am referring to helping your students *construct* knowledge by giving them work worthy of thinking about (Barton 2004; Wharton-McDonald, Pressley, and Hampston 1998). Students need to be involved in worthwhile work to keep them hooked on school. They also need to be successful in school to stay hooked.

So, to teach with rigor is to facilitate the students' construction of knowledge and to reflect on your teaching practices. Reflection is important because it will ensure that you are teaching what students at your grade level need to learn, and because it will push you to grow in your ability to deliver this instruction through purposeful minilessons. When you reflect, you construct knowledge as well; you become a better teacher.

The Importance of Doing *Something*

Perhaps now you are thinking, *So what?* about the notion of moving beyond compliance and creating a connected and cohesive literacy program. It's an honest feeling. I have often worked, talked, and shared with teachers who tell me it is *beyond* them to improve under the sanctions, expectations, and pressures they are facing. Perhaps, like some teachers I've met, you believe that nothing can be done beyond allegiance to a program. Even if you feel this way, I encourage you to take a step back, take a breath, and remember the reason you began teaching in the first place. For me it was to make a difference. I have been the principal of three schools, all of which were identified as program improvement schools at some time. I found the most powerful thing for the staff to do in their quest to improve was to do *something*. Doing something is always a better choice than doing nothing. Align your instruction, assess your students, and teach with purpose and connectedness. Reflect on your work, and strive to tweak it daily to help your students learn. You will become a better teacher no matter what program you are expected to teach.

So. Let's begin the journey and roll out the essentials of teaching reading to children who come to your door with little literacy experience, for whom the same education is not equal education, and who need to be taught explicitly *how* in order to close the achievement gap. May you find inspiration in your students, their incredible abilities, and your potential to teach them well.

CHAPTER TWO

Great Workshops Work

Developing Effective Routines to Teach Struggling Learners

There is a difference between having a good literacy program and having a *great* literacy program. A good literacy program helps children reach grade-level benchmarks through teaching and testing; a *great* literacy program improves student achievement through an integrated process that focuses on showing children how to

- explicitly construct knowledge
- participate in purposeful activities
- make meaning while immersed in language

A great literacy program in a school that serves children of poverty and diversity is focused on ensuring that the children reach grade-level benchmarks, expectations, and standards. Teachers who create and lead these effective programs essentially take children by the hand and show them everything they need to know to be on equal ground with children who do not require as much support to excel at school (Johnson 2002; Pressley et al. 2002; Pressley 2002a).

- Great workshop instruction gives children time to read texts of interest and enjoyment and write on a topic that develops their thinking and knowing.
- Great workshop instruction models reading for children, which leads them to conceptualize and imitate how good readers involve themselves with text.
- Great workshop instruction models thinking about reading and helps children think about and visualize the elements of story, interesting information, and what the story or information means.
- Great workshop instruction is guided by a teacher who leads a program focused on children, their learning, and the best research-based instructional practices.

The best model of workshop instruction connects and integrates opportunities for children to interact with texts while teaching specific strategies to help them become proficient readers (Gaveleck et al. 2000; Pearson and Raphael 2003; Pressley 2000; Taylor, Pearson, et al. 2002). For young children this means that the teacher embeds the basic structures they need to attend to while creating a joyful environment. These structures include decoding, fluency, comprehension, vocabulary development, and concepts of print (Adams 1990; NICHD 2000). In writing, young children learn to encode sounds into words, create meaningful stories, and write simple nonfiction reports (NCEE 2001). Let's take a look at how these ideas would practically work in your classroom.

Workshop Teaching

The structure of reading and writing workshops includes three things:

- the minilesson
- the materials
- the time children spend reading, responding, or writing

An effective workshop takes about an hour. You begin with a minilesson that lasts ten to fifteen minutes; move into the workshop or guided practice, which lasts about forty minutes; and end with a class share that lasts between five and ten minutes. Your instruction will be enhanced if you add a read-aloud, or a language activity, in addition to the workshop. Your daily schedule should flow from focused read-aloud to reading workshop and then to writing workshop. These structures should work together for a cohesive and connected program. Figure 2.1 is an example of Hollie Olsen's second-grade schedule. Hollie teaches at Pinedale Elementary School, where I am the principal. Her classroom is highlighted later in this chapter and in Chapter 11.

FIGURE 2.1 Daily Schedule for Hollie Olsen's Second-Grade Class

Second-Grade Daily Schedule	
8:15–8:30	Greeting and individual skills practice
8:30–9:30	Writing workshop
9:30–10:00	Language development and read-aloud
10:00–10:15	Recess
10:15–11:15	Reading workshop
11:15–11:45	Word study and spelling
11:45–12:35	Lunch
12:35–2:00	Math
2:00–2:30	PE
2:30–3:00	Content studies—social studies and science

How do research-supported elements integrate into this daily schedule? Very easily. Research has a lot to say about reading instruction. It is easy to interpret research as separate sound bites in a literacy program. But the best use of research is to take the strategies, processes, and structures that the studies suggest result in more effective student learning and knit them together into a cohesive program. A cohesive program for the early grades should move children along a literacy continuum from beginners to early fluent readers and writers. This means much more than developing skills in reading and writing. This means that children develop a literate identity and see themselves as successful readers and writers (Clay 2001; Cole 2004).

While the children may be learning skills, they are not aware that they know bits and pieces of information, or discrete skills and facts. Rather, they know they can tackle simple texts with success and write about their life experiences, thoughts, and information and then share this work with others. They make a contribution to the classroom and the world as literate persons. This may sound like a lot to build into the first four formal years in school, but it isn't. Children in third grade have a developing awareness about themselves as readers and writers. We can deliberately enhance this awareness by providing a classroom immersed in language, guided by authentic and purposeful literacy practices, and then hurried by skills instruction that leads children along a developmental continuum *with the purpose* of enhancing their abilities to read and to write and to *see themselves* as readers and writers.

The Literacy Continuum

When organizing your workshops, you have to know where you are going. By developing a perspective of what came before you in the children's literacy development and what comes next, you can effect change by creating a literacy program that moves children forward and prepares them for the next step. During this progression children move from having little understanding of how print works to being fluent readers who are able to read quickly with expression and comprehension (Adams 1990; Clay 2001; Pressley 2002b).

Overall, from kindergarten through third grade, children move through a continuum from simple to complex processing. Professional texts often delineate this movement as changes in a stage. But children are not really moving through a stage. Instead, they are developing a more complex processing of print. To see this continuum clearly, it helps to understand the development of children's processing. The behaviors described in the following framework come from Marie Clay's *Change Over Time in Children's Literacy Development* (2001, 84). (Clay refers to a proficient reader as a child beginning to read texts with greater ability, and a successful reader as a proficient reader at about age eight.)

- *Early*: when a child
  - first becomes aware of print, begins reading print in her environment, and attempts to read simple texts
  - knows a few letters
  - has some concepts of print
  - writes oddly shaped letters and very early books or stories
  - tells a story that might resemble a book
- *Emergent*: when a child
  - begins to connect to some aspects of written language
  - has some understanding of moving left to right and down a page
  - produces many letters, some words, and one or two sentences in writing
  - often uses language in the book to read but often uses own language
  - points, trying to match word by word in reading or while writing
- *Beginner*: when a child
  - can negotiate print with some success
  - knows where to start and where to move in print
  - approaches print word by word in reading and writing
  - knows that texts carry meaning
  - knows pictures can prompt word meaning
  - can focus on and use first and last letters to read words
  - has some success with simple story texts, including texts with two story lines
- *Proficient*: when a child
  - can read across print word by word using syntax as a guide
  - has increased ability to self-correct; notices discrepancies between what was read and the print
  - can predict upcoming words in text based on oral language knowledge or assumptions based on knowledge of the real world
  - sounds out some words, using chunks as well as single letters
- *Fast, accurate processor*: when a child
  - takes ownership for solving new words
  - problem solves new and difficult words and self-corrects many errors
  - integrates information from visual, phonological, semantic, and syntactic understanding
  - processes what is read quickly
  - is able to process information in text quickly
- *Successful*: when a child
  - accurately reads larger chunks of information on more difficult texts
  - develops vocabulary independently
  - problem solves new words and miscued familiar words
  - makes errors that are close to the text's syntactic, visual, phonological, and semantic information

- can alter the amount of attention spent on different knowledge sources, for example, can pay attention to figuring out new words without affecting reading pace
- has a complex structure of processing skills
- reads with effective pace

Children's development as writers mirrors their development as readers (Bear et al. 1996; Templeton and Morris 2000). They move along a continuum from emergent, to beginning, to transitional, and finally to fluent processing. Fluent writers express themselves with voice and style. They are able to write in different genres, and their writing demonstrates a developing ability to use the author's craft and reflect on their work. Spelling ability and orthographic knowledge develop along this continuum as well. Children begin as preliterate, then move through a continuum until they understand how syllables fit together and how words are formed (this understanding is labeled *syllable juncture* and *derivational consistency*). Young children in kindergarten through third grade are developing the following understanding with regard to spelling (Bear et al. 1996):

- *Preliterate spelling*: when a child
  - writes with no sound-symbol correspondence
  - may scribble or draw for writing
  - may use some letters, but confuse them with others that sound or look alike, such as *b* and *p*
- *Early letter name spelling*: when a child
  - uses several letters of the alphabet
  - writes syllabically using the most prominent features of the word
  - uses most beginning and ending consonants
  - develops clear letter-sound correspondences
- *Within-word-pattern spelling*: when a child between the ages of six and twelve
  - uses most letters of the alphabet when spelling
  - has clear letter-sound correspondences
  - may not control correct letter-sound correspondences based on how he hears the word

While children's development moves forward along this continuum, it is framed by what they know and can do correctly, what they can do but not consistently, and what they don't know how to do. Our instruction during our literacy block (which includes reading and writing workshop and direct instruction in word work, language, and shared reading, which are discussed in later chapters) focuses on moving children toward fluent reading and writing. Great workshop teachers give feedback and instruction based on what children know, what they are beginning to understand, and what they don't know.

Children develop some skills and strategies by working with text and language in the workshop; they learn other skills when given direct instruction and practice time. In effective workshops, skills taught through direct instruction are designed to move children forward as rapidly as possible along the literacy continuum. The more effective workshop teachers teach the skills children need to know in a systematic way but do so by focusing on *skill* application rather than *synthetic* applications. Synthetic applications are made-up or tightly controlled skills practice, which are often focused on a worksheet (McGee and Richgels 2003; NICHD 2000).

Create your workshop routines and structures around essential elements that are supported by research. Research-based practices that will support your reading workshop include (Mazzoni and Gambrell 2003; Mesmer and Griffith 2006; Pressley 2002b)

- teaching reading for meaning-making literacy experiences
- integrating a comprehensive word study (phonics) program into reading and writing instruction
- giving direct instruction in decoding and comprehension strategies
- using multiple texts that link and expand concepts and strategies
- building a whole-class community that emphasizes concept development
- creating time for children to read in class
- teaching small-group reading while the other children read and write about what they have read
- using a variety of assessments to monitor student progress and tailor instruction

Showing Is Not a Worksheet

I began this chapter by highlighting how great workshop instruction helps children learn. I also stressed that the teacher is a leader. Leading means you are active. There will be things your children need to learn directly from you, times you need to provide direct instruction. This is much more effective when you don't change your focus or goal of purposeful and authentic instruction but instead use this goal to enhance your overall program. You don't have to stop and pull out a worksheet on the *-ap* spelling pattern. You can teach the spelling pattern in a directed lesson in which children brainstorm words, work with the words on a whiteboard while gathered in the meeting area, and then refer to the posted words during writing workshop to figure out how to spell a word or refer to the chart when decoding a word while reading. In fact, you will need to model *many times* how to use a new skill. If you were to visit Pinedale Elementary School, you would see teachers integrating skills seamlessly into the workshop. You might hear teachers say things like this:

- "If you know the *-ap* chunk, then you know *nap* and *lap*."
- "Look at how we chunk the word *breakfast*."

- "Wow, Sarah just went back and reread the word she sounded out. Good readers go back and reread."

Your classroom should provide ample opportunities for guided practice while you sit nearby and watch a child read or write. Then, when it is appropriate, you may choose to use a worksheet to reinforce learning. The workshop curriculum should drive the use of worksheets; worksheets should not drive the focus of a workshop. Effective classrooms show children what they need to know and how to practice by modeling. Direct instruction balanced with carefully constructed *workshops* ensures student learning.

The Focused Literacy Block: One Example

Hollie Olsen is a second-grade teacher at Pinedale Elementary School. She works very closely with her teaching partner, Pam Pflepsen. Together Hollie and Pam have created an integrated literacy block focused on extensive work in reading workshop. Hollie's and Pam's children read well by the time they leave their classrooms. In fact, all of the children at Pinedale Elementary School excel in the primary grades. While as a school team, we gather qualitative data on how children are progressing on the literacy continuum, the test results of the annual summative assessments have shown substantial student growth over time. While the following schedule is used in Hollie's second-grade classroom, the first-grade and third-grade classrooms at the school follow the same framework. However, the kindergarten schedule has been modified (see Figure 2.2), since kindergarten is in session for only three and a half hours.

FIGURE 2.2 Kindergarten Daily Schedule

Kindergarten Daily Schedule

8:00–8:20	Welcome; independent skills centers
8:20–8:50	Circle time (whole-class language teaching, including read-aloud, shared reading, interactive writing, phonics, vocabulary development, class news, and calendar)
8:50–9:50	Centers, including reading instruction and writing center
9:50–10:15	Reading workshop (consisting of a read-aloud and time for children to respond in writing)
10:15–10:30	Recess and snack
10:30–10:50	Math
10:50–11:20	Writing

8:15–8:30 *Morning Skill Exercises on Vocabulary and Word Work*

While Hollie greets each child individually, collects homework, and checks attendance, the children apply their developing knowledge by working on their practice sheets. So much of the children's day is spent on activities that support divergent thinking and response that it is critical for them to spend a few minutes finding the one right answer. Knowing how to do this is a life skill.

It is also a skill students need to score well on the district's annual standards assessment. These few minutes spent practicing are important for the children so that they will not be at a disadvantage when taking tests. While it is not an appropriate approach to Hollie's entire literacy program, if she spends a few minutes in the morning on developing this skill, while she is busy preparing for the day, it will be time well spent for her class.

8:30–9:30 *Writing Workshop*

Writing workshop begins with the children gathered on the floor in the class meeting area. A cozy rug delineates the space, an inviting box of books is stashed nearby, and a rocking chair sits next to an easel. The area is surrounded by picture books, word lists, and teaching charts the class has created. The area is engaging and full of purpose. Hollie begins her lesson. While she talks about writing, she moves from posing the idea and information for the day to modeling how to write and use the strategy she is teaching. Then she pauses for a minute or two for the children to share with a partner.

After the minilesson the children leave the area and settle in at their desks to write. Each child has a writing folder to organize his writing. Several children visit the writing area, where extra paper and pencils are stored. The children are independent. They don't come to Hollie and ask repeatedly what they need to do. They know this is their time to write, and they jump right in. Hollie moves around the room, conferring with students. She winds up the one-hour writing workshop with a share time. The children join her on the floor again.

The instruction includes several research-based strategies. Hollie employs a variety of strategies that she subtly tucks into her workshop, including

- using visuals during the minilesson
- focusing on a singular message
- modeling how to apply the writing in order to think and comprehend during minilesson and conferring
- ensuring guided practice for thirty minutes during the workshop
- engaging the emotional needs of the children during conferring and minilesson
- providing immediate, effective, and nurturing feedback during conferring

9:30–10:00 Language Development and Read-Aloud

The children gather on the floor of the group area to listen to and discuss a picture book Hollie has read earlier. The titles of other books the children have read grace the walls near the floor, where Hollie has displayed copies of the covers of the books she has read aloud to the class. Children are reminded of their work as a group and their learning when they glance at the titles. Hollie focuses on the vocabulary in the book. She also wants children to become independent and learn to think about a book. Hollie uses this time for the children to turn and discuss with partners what they think is happening in the book and why.

10:00–10:15 Recess

10:15–11:15 Reading Workshop

Hollie doesn't have the children visit reading stations or centers. The children spend thirty to forty minutes reading and responding to their reading in journals. Hollie begins the workshop with a minilesson that clearly focuses the children's attention on the strategy or skill she is teaching. Then the children are off to work with their book boxes (for more information on book boxes, see page 22 in Chapter 3). About twenty-five minutes into the workshop, Hollie reminds children to begin their reading responses. The children move from reading to writing about their reading.

During the workshop Hollie is either working with guided reading groups or conferring. During guided reading, Hollie supports children as they attempt a text that they can almost read on their own but not quite. She teaches a reading strategy, often a fix-up or decoding strategy, and then guides or coaches the children through their reading of the text. Hollie alternates guided reading with conferring with children one-on-one; during a

---

Why Reading and Writing Workshop?

You may be wondering how to explain your reasoning for teaching authentic reading and writing through a workshop rather than more traditional teaching strategies to your administrator, colleagues, or students' parents. You don't need to face any of these conversations with queasiness if your choices are grounded in research and results. There is a lot of research that suggests best practices in reading and writing instruction, and as a busy teacher, it can be difficult to find the time to wade through the literature yourself. If you need backup to explain your choices for teaching reading, there are many insightful articles in *What Research Has to Say About Reading Instruction*, edited by Alan E. Farstrup and S. Jay Samuels (2002), that can be useful. Two books that can provide research to inform your writing workshop are *The Art of Teaching Writing*, by Lucy Calkins (1994), and *Writing: Teachers and Children at Work*, by Donald Graves (2003). If your administrator requests additional information, I recommend the section titled "Literacy Education: The Greatest Opportunity of All" in *Results Now: How We Can Achieve Unprecedented Improvements in Teaching and Learning*, by Mike Schmoker (2006).

conference she listens to the child read, records notes about his progress (often by taking a running record), and gives the child a reading goal before moving on. Hollie uses these conferences to check that the child has the correct books in his book box, is using reading strategies independently, and isn't frustrated or bored with books that are too hard or too easy.

11:15–11:45   Word Study

Next, Hollie explicitly teaches *how* words are put together and models *how* to think about figuring out words when reading and spelling. The goal of this explicit instruction is twofold: she wants children to be confident in their ability to figure out how to pronounce words while reading and how to spell words while writing. Because her teaching style and classroom atmosphere drench children in literacy, word study is the second time of the day when she teaches a few skills. She wants to ensure that children know and understand various word patterns and word roots. Hollie's lessons are based on a whole-to-part approach to word learning. The children are practicing skills that focus on how print works, the structure of language, conventions, and letter-sound relationships. This is the part of the day when Hollie introduces her spelling words for the week. Her lists are grouped around a spelling pattern, or onset and rime; sight words; or a decoding skill. The children are focused on individual words that are grouped together based on spelling patterns.

Leading with Vision

This chapter has focused on leading your workshops with purpose and vision. Workshop instruction is effective when it is guided by focused instruction. Struggling children need us to teach literacy with precision—to lead, teach explicitly, and provide guided practice through authentic application. This may not be news to you, and you may wonder why I have repeated this theme many times. You probably have a workshop or some type of reading block set up in your classroom, you probably are moving children along a continuum of literacy development, you probably are facing the public accountability measures from your district or state with ease, so why change?

Change is necessary because many children continue to enter upper grades reading at least one year behind (Hiebert and Taylor 2000; Klenk and Kibby 2000). Effective, thoughtful workshop instruction, however, ensures children will learn and eventually catch up. In effective workshops, teachers provide the following (Fountas and Pinnell 2006; Pressley 2002b):

- a clear objective in a ten- or fifteen-minute minilesson
- practice in reading and writing with actual texts, not with worksheets
- short, direct instruction supported by visuals instead of lecture
- feedback during the workshop through conferring and through coaching during guided reading

Well-developed workshops provide monitoring with feedback, avoid lecture, and don't rely on worksheets for guided practice (Calkins 2001). More important, workshops begin with a minilesson that has a clear objective that models and reveals the thinking of a fluent reader: the teacher. Find a partner or a team you can work with. Together you can create a reading workshop that meets the high demands of teaching children who need support.

CHAPTER THREE

The Reading Workshop
The Essential Components

Corinne contacted me after a workshop I had recently given on reading comprehension instruction. She asked if she could visit Pinedale Elementary School so that she could see firsthand how the issues and ideas I discussed in the reading seminar were implemented in the classroom. She hoped we could help her set up a reading workshop in her classroom and overcome some of the hurdles she faced trying to implement it alone.

Having Corinne come as a visitor was a pleasure; collaborating makes us tick at our school, and inviting a colleague from another school was a welcome diversion. On the day of Corinne's visit I met her in the front office; she was bubbling with the excitement of learning something new. I, too, felt excited; each time a new person comes through the school door is an opportunity for us to improve our craft. Often, when we see ourselves through someone else's eyes, we can see what our next steps should be. Corinne stayed for the entire morning block. I met her again after recess. She grabbed my arm and said, "I need to know how to do this. I need to know how to teach like this, make my classroom work well for children and have literacy, beautiful literacy, be at the core of what I do. *How* do I do this?"

Corinne's passionate question made me realize that I often forget the first steps to starting a reading workshop in the classroom. I forget that when you are working on this alone or with a couple of teaching partners, it is hard to see where to begin. Sometimes this is challenging, because you have to redesign your room and take the risk of teaching something new or teaching reading in a new way. Doing something new is always hard.

The Reading Workshop Structure

Setting up a reading workshop doesn't have to be difficult. While there is so much more depth to teaching reading than I am going to attempt to explain, I hope this chapter will guide you through the beginning steps. Effective workshop instruction is broken into four major sections (Calkins 2001; Fountas and Pinnell 2000; see Figure 3.1):

- minilesson
- reading work
- written response to reading
- share and wrap-up

The Minilesson

The minilesson is how you launch the workshop. A minilesson is a short lesson (about fifteen minutes) during which you provide direct instruction focused on one objective, model your thinking, and then explain to children how a strategy, idea, or information will help them learn during the workshop.

FIGURE 3.1 Components of Reading Workshop

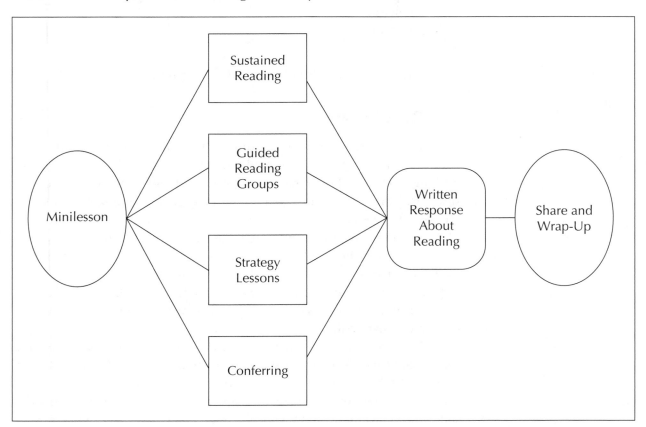

What the Minilesson Might Look Like

Lori Garcia-Higgs has gathered her students in her class meeting area. These first graders are intent and watching her closely. They know it is time to begin reading workshop and their job is to listen and to think.

Lori focuses their attention. "We have been working so hard during the last few weeks sharing our favorite parts in the stories we are reading. We have written about our favorite parts, drawn pictures of our favorite parts, and shared our favorite parts with our friends in room 5." Lori pauses to point at a chart hanging nearby. The chart is titled "Favorite Part," and several children's written responses are hung underneath the title.

"So today, we are going to write and share our connections! I know this is new, but we have been talking about our connections for *weeks*! Today you are going to write about a connection that you make in a book while you are reading. Let me show you how I made a connection this morning to one of my favorite books, *Toot and Puddle: Charming Opal* [Hobbie 2003a]."

The children clap their hands as Lori pulls *Toot and Puddle: Charming Opal* out of the "Favorites" basket, which is located under the easel next to her chair. Lori has just launched the minilesson. She continues the lesson as she walks the children carefully through her thinking. Her lesson consists of four parts:

- the connection
- direct instruction
- engagement
- closure

(See Chapter 6 for more information on minilessons.)

The Reading Work

The reading work is the actual reading children do each day, and they need to do a lot of it. Children should be reading real books more often and for longer periods of time than we might think they should. In fact, activities or *stuff* doesn't need to be part of our classroom. Stuff might include worksheet-driven activities like coloring, tracing, crafts, and fill-in-the-blank tasks. Art, painting, and drawing need to move to a time of day when they can be honored for what they are: creative expression and the nurturing of artistic development. Too often, our reading block is filled with activities that don't nurture reading. Children still draw in our reading workshops in response to reading. But be careful; reluctant writers will draw more than write.

While it may seem drastic to say *stop the activities*, arranging lots of time for our children to spend in sustained reading is essential. If an activity is in your daily schedule because it takes time up in your day, and it doesn't further students' ability to read, then don't do it. The children who attend Pinedale Elementary come from a neighborhood that has been immersed in poverty for many years. While each child is precious and brings her unique perspective to the classroom, it is honest to recognize that the children who fill our classroom each day need us to lead their literacy learning. They need us to recognize detractors, say *enough* to extra activities, and focus their time in school on learning. During reading work, children are reading independently with a purpose or participating in guided reading, transitional guided reading, or individual conferences.

What the Reading Work Might Look Like

Lori reached across the round reading table. "Give me a high five!" she told José. José looked up at her with a grin spreading ear to ear. He quickly returned the gesture and their hands spanked in the air. José giggled.

"I *love* the way you went back to your text and *thought about* your connection. You did what great readers do, just like we talked about in the minilesson! How does it feel, José?"

José looked up at Lori and nodded vigorously. "Great! I like my connection."

"Great! When it is time to write your response, make sure to write *all* of your thinking on the response sheet. Let's put a sticky note on the page in the book where you made your connection." José watched Lori intently as she grabbed a sticky note from her supply box. He smiled a big smile. After this quick reinforcement from Lori, José scampered back to his special reading area and dove into his reading.

Lori glanced beyond the group gathered at the reading table. The children were reading, and they were intent. They were spread about the room, all working on their reading. Books were pulled out of the book boxes; stacks of high-interest books or old favorites sat near the easel in an accessible place. The atmosphere was charged with the thoughts of many children reading at one time.

The Structure of Reading Work

Lori begins the workshop with the minilesson. After the minilesson, the children leave the floor meeting area one by one, gather their reading materials, find a special spot in the room, and begin to read. The children are focused and engaged. It is as if they are on a mission to read and enjoy, to think about their reading and share their thinking with a nearby friend.

The children read for thirty to forty minutes. The purpose of this focused time is twofold: first, to develop reading *stamina* while practicing skills and strategies and, second, to give children much-needed time to read independently. Reading stamina is important. The more children read books consistent with their reading level, the better they will be able to sit and read for several minutes at a time without getting distracted. I call this "bottom time": children need to develop the length of time they can stay on their bottom with a book, or several books, and read. Most children who cannot sustain a period of reading have never had the opportunity to read, every day, with a set of books at their reading level.

Reading work is organized by the book box, which is simply a cardboard or plastic box that fits on a shelf and is easily carried around by a young child (magazine boxes work best). What you place in the box for each child makes a world of difference. If you choose the books well, and create a system for the children to self-select their own books well, the book box will help you manage the workshop. Figure 3.2 shows the book boxes in Lori's room. She stores them on a shelf when they are not in use.

A well-outfitted book box will allow children to

- have plenty of material to read with interest for at least thirty minutes
- engage with high-interest books
- practice reading instructional-level books carefully chosen by the teacher
- practice reading self-selected books at their independent reading level
- practice decoding and comprehension strategies they have learned during guided reading and word work

The book box is filled with

- leveled texts at independent and instructional levels
- high-interest fiction and nonfiction
- library books
- word rings (for information on word rings, see page 105 in Chapter 8)
- shared reading poetry books
- a reading response journal
- textbooks (if you don't have access to lots of reading materials)

FIGURE 3.2 Book Boxes in Lori's Classroom

Reading work is split between just-right books (which include books at a child's instructional level) and high-interest books. High-interest books are trade books and picture books that children choose on their own. These books may not be at their reading level, but are old favorites, class mentor texts, or content books that the children want to read because they are interesting and fun. During first- and second-grade reading workshops, the teachers at Pinedale tell the children when to switch books, to ensure that children are practicing their reading for at least twenty minutes in leveled texts before they turn to high-interest books.

Why Just-Right Books Are Important

While it may seem limiting to control how long the children read a particular set of books, remember that the goal is to give the children time to practice reading books that have been specifically chosen for them. The book box includes books that are *just right*, which means that the child's thinking muscles are getting good exercise. Children should be working their brain when reading, just slightly, not too much. They should be trying out strategies they have learned at the guided reading table or during whole-class read-alouds. Reading should feel *almost* easy to the children, automatically reinforcing the time they spend reading. These books should be fun and enjoyable for the students.

Instructional-Level Books Are Bridges

There are also a few instructional-level books in the book box. These books are just right for children as well. Instructional-level books are matched to students' reading ability based on the results of a running record or a Development Reading Assessment (DRA). At an instructional level, children read 90 to 94 percent of the words correctly (Fountas and Pinnell 1996). These books should make them think just a bit harder while reading. You should see the children actively using reading strategies to read these books. These should be texts you have shown them in guided reading. Most important, these books should help them make the transition to the next stage in their reading development. Think about this transition like a bridge. You are bridging the children from one text level to the next with the books you are giving them to read (see Figure 3.3) and by simultaneously keeping them excited and interested in reading. The effort necessary to read these instructional-level books should motivate them to keep going, not crush their spirit.

The children in your room should start off reading just-right books at their independent reading level. As the year goes on, slip a few instructional books into the mix (after instruction in guided reading), thus providing a smooth transition between levels.

What Reading a Just-Right Book Might Look Like

Karina sits with legs dangling; her feet do not touch the floor but move round and round as she concentrates with her brow furrowed. In her hands

FIGURE 3.3

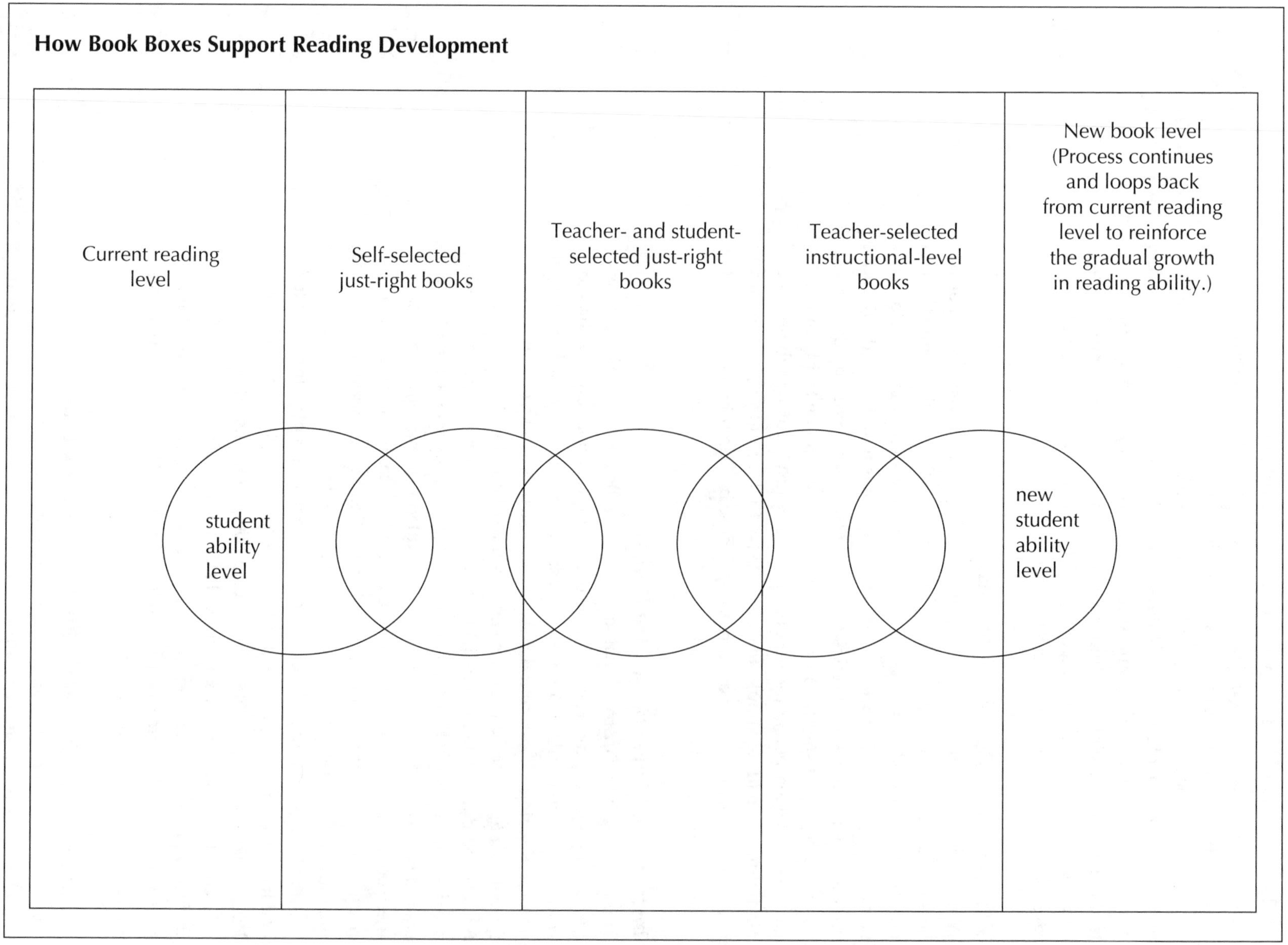

How Book Boxes Support Reading Development

Current reading level	Self-selected just-right books	Teacher- and student-selected just-right books	Teacher-selected instructional-level books	New book level (Process continues and loops back from current reading level to reinforce the gradual growth in reading ability.)

student ability level

new student ability level

she grips *Chico* (Almada 2004), a book designated as level C on the Rigby guided reading text gradient. She lays the book down on the table in front of her, leans forward with her reading finger (right index finger) ready, and begins to point under each word on the page, "Chico . . . can . . . sit." She comes to a word she is unsure of—*shake*—and purses her lips.

"Get your mouth ready," Lori says as she leans forward and taps her finger on the word.

Karina looks at the word for a moment, forms the /sh/ sound and says, "Shake." She looks up at Lori, beaming.

"Wow! Karina, you figured out that word all on your own!" Lori says.

During partner reading, Karina is sitting on the reading carpet reading an old favorite from the class book box to her partner, Hope. The girls laugh and giggle and look intently at the pictures in the book. Then Karina lays the book aside and pulls out *Farm Alarm* (Bryson 2003) from her book box. This is a book Karina received during guided reading instruction a week before. She reads, placing her reading finger under each word. She shows Hope the pictures. She comes to the word *asleep* and hesitates for a moment. She purses her lips, says the /ah/ sound under her breath, and then says "asleep." Before going on, she goes back and rereads the sentence *Sheep was asleep* without hesitation.

Written Response to Reading

The children have been reading for about a half hour. It is quiet, but a hum that has broken out in one corner of the room is growing in momentum. This natural hum signals that the children are coming up for air. They have been reading nonstop and are beginning to look about the room and share their reading with friends. Sometimes they share things a bit off topic too, but that is normal—all readers do this from time to time. This moment helps children mentally regroup and prepare to work a bit longer; it is a natural time to help young children shift from reading to responding to a reading.

For first graders this occurs anywhere between twenty and thirty minutes into the workshop; for second and third graders it occurs after the children read a bit longer, about thirty to forty minutes. In kindergarten the ebb and flow of centers defines this time in a slightly different way. Some kindergarten teachers run a twenty-minute reading workshop separate from their center time. Others create a center where the children read and respond to their reading.

During reading response the children respond to their reading by writing in a notebook or on a response sheet. What they write about is directed by the focus of the minilesson. It is important that they spend time recording their thoughts, because the process of thinking and writing deepens their comprehension of the book and gives them practice with reading and writing strategies (Galda, Ash, and Cullinan 2000).

character in Leo Lionni's book *Alexander and the Wind-Up Mouse* (1969). His writing says: *I was thinking when the mouse went to chase the wind-up mouse maybe he just wanted him to be like him*. Notice what Jeremy has learned about responding to books and how to write about his ideas. He keeps his writing focused on his book response, stretches some words to write them phonetically, and spells a few sight words correctly.

First-Grade Reading Response: Focus on Comprehension

First-grade reading response expands and guides student thinking about comprehension. While first graders can respond to books read aloud, this is when they begin to respond to books they read on their own during reading workshop. After watching their teacher provide explicit instruction during the minilesson on how to think about books, comprehend text, and write about thinking, children are ready to dive in and try out reading response independently. When children read and then respond, they are focused simultaneously on both comprehension and decoding. The smart and effective workshop teacher knows that asking higher-order questions and emphasizing writing to respond to reading helps children become readers (Pearson and Duke 2002). This is what first graders do in the workshop. This is why they begin reading response right away, on the first day of school!

Reading response in first grade is guided by the overall theme of your unit of study. In the beginning of the year the children may respond by drawing a picture of their favorite part of the story; by the end of the year they may produce a retelling, a story element analysis, a character analysis, or a description of their mental images. First graders can respond on plain paper, lined paper stapled into booklets, or response frames. How you choose to have children respond depends on what you model in the minilesson. Some of the responses may be written in paragraph form, others as graphs. A simple way to prepare response journals is to take a few pieces of wide-lined paper and staple them together beneath a construction paper cover. Figure 3.5 shows a few examples of response journals. These booklets are excellent records of the children's comprehension development progress.

Ray was a student in Sonia Velo's first-grade classroom at Lee Richmond School, in Hanford, California. Sonia had been working with the children for some time on how to make text-to-self connections. In January of first grade Ray read *Baby Bear's Present*, by Beverley Randell (1996; see Figure 3.6, p. 29). On page 11 Ray made a text-to-self connection (see Figures 3.7 and 3.8, p. 30). He wrote: *baby bear's present. He wanted a car. This book reminds me when I wanted a car too. His car was blue mine was red*. Notice how Ray marked the page with a sticky note. He placed a small sticky note under the words that made him think of his connection, and then he wrote his thinking on the paper.

FIGURE 3.5 Response Journals

FIGURE 3.6 Front Cover of *Baby Bear's Present*

FIGURE 3.7 Page 11 of *Baby Bear's Present*

"No! No!" said Baby Bear.

"I like the blue car.

  I can make it go.

  I can go for rides in it.

  Please let me have the car."

▮▮▮▮▮▮ Bear said,

"I like the train."

11

FIGURE 3.8 Ray's Reading Response

Sara was also in Sonia's classroom. She read *Lizard Loses His Tail*, by Beverley Randell (2004a; see Figure 3.9). Sara worked to stretch each sound as she wrote her response (see Figure 3.10, p. 32). Her response isn't as easy to read, but it shows what Sara was thinking as she read: *Today I read a book about Lizard loses his tail and my lizard loses his tail too. Lizard loses his tail.* Sara knew that she needed to make a text connection, and hers almost sounds made up! She wasn't able to extend her thinking; she was able only to copy the words down from the book. Some first graders will take longer than others to develop their ability to respond in a single thought about a book. Although Sara did not elaborate on her idea, she was able to make a connection and keep her writing to one point.

First graders and reading response paper

One way to guide first-grade reading response is by using the response frames I mentioned earlier. First-grade response papers that work well begin with large spaces for drawing and a few lines for writing and then move toward paper with only lines. The paper does encourage the child to write, and paper with more lines will encourage more thinking. However, paper with lots of lines can also encourage children simply to fill up the lines with repetitive phrases or connected sentences. Of course, it isn't very purposeful for a child to write a bunch of words that don't really say anything (and first graders can do this well sometimes—writing *I like the rainbow* over and over, for example), but it also isn't purposeful not to provide first graders the opportunity to write more. Often the paper choices we

FIGURE 3.9 Front Cover of *Lizard Loses His Tail*

FIGURE 3.10 Sara's Reading Response

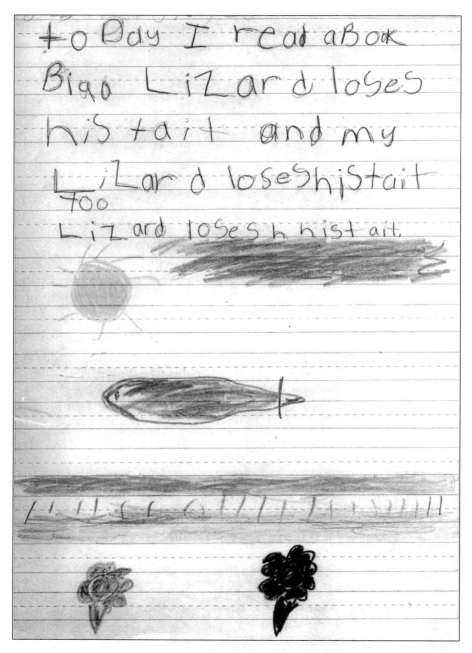

offer unconsciously tell children what we think they can do. There are full-size black-line masters of several paper choices in the Appendix.

In his response to a book he has read titled *Ten Little Garden Snails* (Randell 2004; see Figure 3.11), Trey is using a *book response* frame. The frame asks him only to write his name, the book title, and a short sentence. Trey writes: *This book reminded me when GG had snails in her plant and she took them out and she stepped on them and I found one and I stepped on it.*

FIGURE 3.11 Trey's Response Using a Response Frame

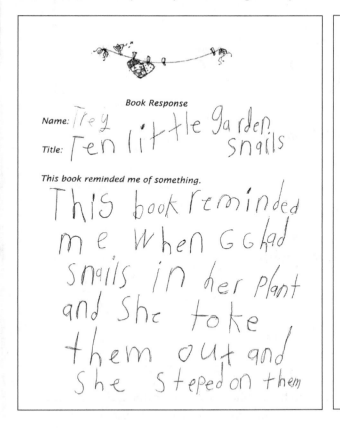

Book Response

Name: Trey

Title: Ten little garden snails

This book reminded me of something.

This book reminded me when GG had snails in her plant and she toke them out and she steped on them

and I found one and I stepedon it.

Figure 3.12 (p. 34) uses the same book response frame, which focuses on writing a text connection. Here, Jasmine is responding to *Sally and the Sparrows*, by Jenny Giles (1997). She writes: *It reminded me when I heard a sound, woke up and it was outside. There were sparrows. I told them to calm down. They didn't. I said, "Are you hungry?" They made that sound. "Enough," I said.* Jasmine's response is more detailed and developed than the other first-grade examples.

Response frames give you the opportunity to differentiate reading response instruction as needed; they also act as an instant assessment tool for noting children's progress. Because you are guiding *how* children respond, you can note their progress on an assigned or self-selected structure.

Second- and Third-Grade Reading Response: Focus on Strategy-Based Responses

Second and third graders need to expand their thinking about books, so their writing changes. The focus is *not* on developing a well-written response to literature, but rather on having the children learn to think and express their thoughts on a book using a research-based reading strategy (see Chapter 6 for more on strategies). I have met many second- and third-grade teachers who worried that the need for children to write well on fourth- or fifth-grade

FIGURE 3.12 Jasmine's Response Using a Response Frame

Book Response

Name: Jasmine

Title: Sally and the Sparrows

This book reminded me of something.

Wen I hrd a saoo I wok yp I hrd sparoows. I tud tne to cum then Wr sparoows. It reminoes my dan tenn Dint i seto or you MG-y they mao rat saoo ucern i seo whst act sieo

assessments drove the need to have children write about reading in second grade. While this may be true in some test-driven schools, the real truth is that young children need to write in order to *think*, and very young children should be given the opportunity to respond to and write about their reading. The process of writing and responding guides children to memorialize their thoughts and opinions about what they read. It is also an active walk-through of a reading strategy modeled in a minilesson.

The writing gives them a way to purposefully practice a skill or strategy that good readers use. Notice that in the three following pieces from early in the school year, the second graders write about their text connections. Their writing reveals their understanding of how to respond to books in specific ways.

Figure 3.13 is Mikaela's short retelling of the book she read, *The Kick-a-Lot Shoes*, by Joy Cowley (2001): *Today I read* The Kick-a-Lot Shoes, *story by Joy Cowley. The old witch kicked people. And the people kicked her as she can't sit down.* Retelling is a simple way for children to respond to texts they read.

Second graders and reading response paper
Second graders need to extend their thinking and write deeper. The graphic organizers available to them should reflect this need. By second grade children often use sticky notes to guide their thinking and comprehension of text. Sometimes the children see the act of writing on the sticky notes as the point of the exercise; they don't understand that using a sticky note is a way

FIGURE 3.13 Mikaela's Writing

Today i read The Kick-a-Lot Shoes, Story by Joy Cowly. The old witch kicked people. And the people kicked her as she can't sit down.

to help them comprehend better. Hollie (the second-grade teacher you met in Chapter 2) created a response paper that works well for children to record their thinking. She made a space on the side where they can put a sticky note. The sticky note is filled with their jots from the reading. The sticky note reminds the children of what they were thinking while reading and makes it easier for them to remember important points for their response writing. This response frame (see page 192) and several others are available in the appendix.

Making a text-to-self connection and retelling are both reading strategies. Research tells us that children who comprehend text well make connections between what they are reading and their own lives and memories. Children who read well are also able to remember what they have read. Second graders Dominque and Jazlynn wrote text-to-self connections in response to the texts they read (see Figures 3.14 and 3.15, pp. 36–37). Dominique also read *The Kick-a-Lot Shoes*, by Joy Cowley: *My connection is a*

FIGURE 3.14 Dominque's Writing

witch and she likes to kick people because she likes to kick people and she thinks it is funny. When I kick my brother my brother kicks me back. Jazlynn read *Amelia Bedelia*, by Peggy Parish (1992). She wrote: *This reminds me of when my pie was burning in the kitchen. I had to make another pie. I had to put ingredients for the pie. I had to go to the store to buy food only for the pie.*

FIGURE 3.15 Jazlynn's Writing

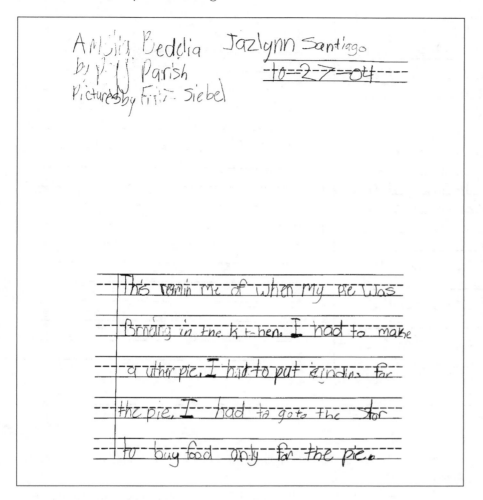

Amelia Bedelia   Jazlynn Santiago
by P.J. Parish   10-27-04
Pictures by Fritz Siebel

This remind me of when my pie was
Brning in the kt-hen. I had to make
a uther pie. I had to put ejndins for
the pie. I had to go to the stor
to buy food only for the pie.

As children learn to extend their thinking and develop comprehension strategies, they will begin reading more difficult texts and will have more to write about during reading response. Figure 3.16 (p. 38) is an example of second grader Carlos' reading response in November. He had read *Horrible Harry and the Green Slime*, by Suzy Kline (1998), and made a text-to-world connection. Not only was he able to explain the connection and the similarities between the book and the cartoon, but he was also able to contrast them by stating one difference. He wrote: *Today I read Horrible Harry and the Green Slime. It reminds me of Scooby-Doo! When Scooby, Shaggy, Velma, Daphne, and Freddy were chasing a monster with green slime on it. In the book Horrible Harry has green slime, too. One is a book and the other one is a cartoon on Cartoon Network. There are lots of Scooby-Doo movies, too. And in Horrible Harry and the Green Slime there is slime in room 2B. That's Harry's classroom. But, there is one thing different about Scooby Doo and Horrible Harry and the Green Slime. On*

FIGURE 3.16 Carlos' Response Piece

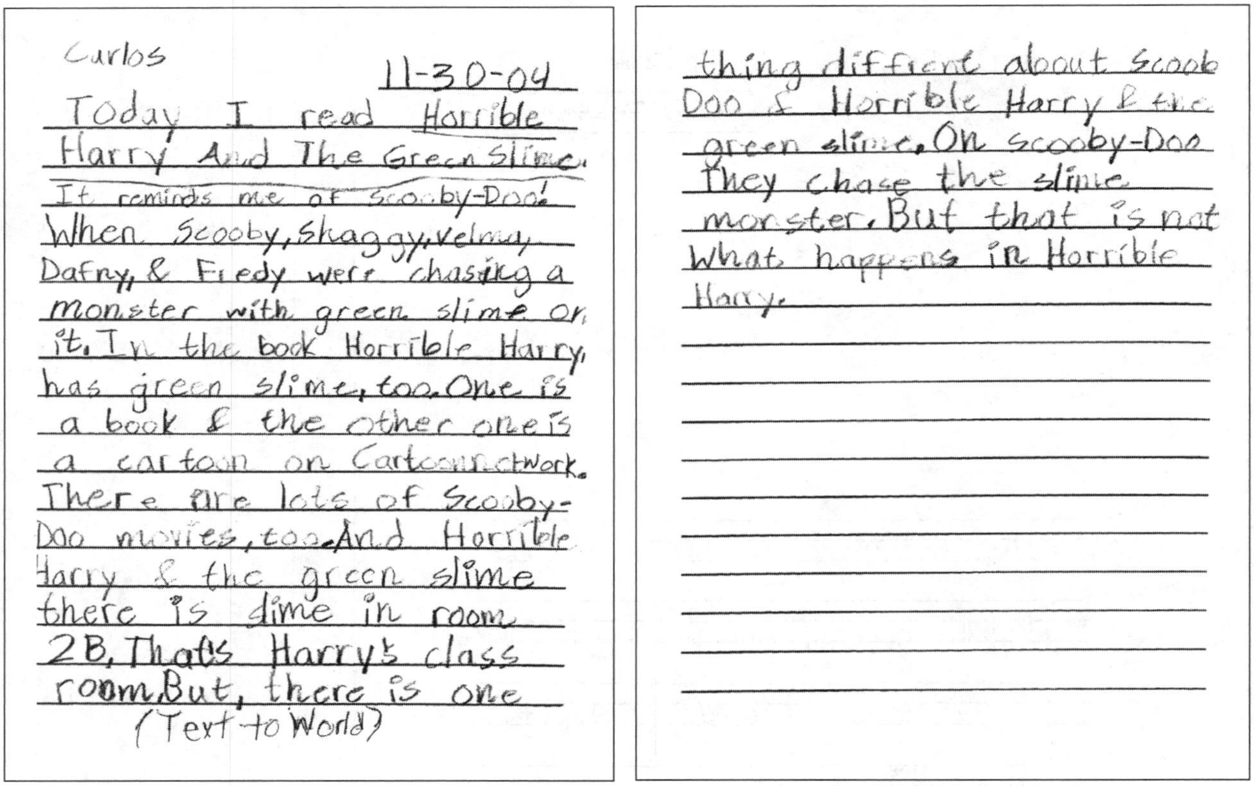

Carlos
11-30-04
Today I read Horrible Harry And The Green Slime. It reminds me of Scooby-Doo! When Scooby, Shaggy, Velma, Dafny, & Fredy were chasing a monster with green slime on it. In the book Horrible Harry, has green slime, too. One is a book & the other one is a cartoon on Cartoon network. There are lots of Scooby-Doo movies, too. And Horrible Harry & the green slime there is slime in room 2B. That's Harry's class room. But, there is one
(Text to World)

thing diffrent about Scoob Doo & Horrible Harry & the green slime. On Scooby-Doo they chase the slime monster. But that is not what happens in Horrible Harry.

Scooby-Doo they chase the slime monster. But that is not what happens in Horrible Harry.

Stacey wrote a text-to-self connection in January of second grade (see Figure 3.17). Stacey thought she was making a text-to-world connection because she was discussing moving and she thought she mentioned how people moved in general, but she lapsed into a text-to-self connection. The significance of this example is Stacey's thinking. She understood a lot about text connections and the piece she read. She developed this knowledge in a short time in second grade, as she had not experienced reading workshop or a focus on comprehension strategies prior to second grade. While she needs to refine her thinking, her piece is an excellent example of the length and quantity you can expect second graders to produce.

Third graders and reading response paper
Third graders are on the move and writing in their own in notebooks! Third grade is the year to begin transitioning children from the copied paper with lines and boxes to lined paper in notebooks. Third graders have a bit more maturity. They can hold their pencils properly and with ease; they are able to form letters more quickly; and overall they need less space to write. They

FIGURE 3.17 Stacey's Reading Response

> 1-11-05
>
> Today I read the book Iris and Walter by Elissa Haden Guest today I made a text to world connection. When Iris is moving that reminds me of when I was moving to my dad's house I was sad and in the book of Iris and Iris was mad because there were no children in the city. That reminds me when had no friends but then I made one friend and it was a she it was fun because she is nice. Iris was sad because there was no children in the city they play all kinds of games. like rollar skating and ride on ponys. like counting stars. Play hind-and-seek. Walter showed his collection of hats. When I come from my house I play with her we dress up in costumes. We play Disney games like snow white. We put Disney snacks.

are becoming conscious of themselves as independent thinkers, so it is only natural that they begin using notebooks to record their responses. Any type of notebook works well. Spiral-bound notebooks tend to wear out quickly, becasuse third graders are still a bit tough on materials. So don't expect them to last all year. You may want to purchase spiral-bound notebooks with only a few pages so that after the children fill one up, they can receive a new notebook.

While most third graders may zoom on in notebooks, third graders who are new to English benefit from the frames used in kindergarten and first and second grades to support and guide their thinking. Graphic organizers help frame their thinking around a particular response and guide their thinking through the response writing. You can support their thinking and comprehension by using reading response papers that match the reading comprehension study you are working on.

You don't have to use a certain type of paper in your reading workshop, but you can support student learning through the scaffold that a *selection* of paper provides. Paper choice may seem like a small thing to think about, but it is important. When you are working toward increasing student learning and meeting accountability expectations, you have to scaffold thinking and writing strategies for children. If a frame encourages a particular type of response, one that children need to learn, if it helps children think about their reading and then write a response that increases their comprehension, then the frame is purposeful.

If providing special paper or a frame for children's writing bothers you, then don't do it; simply provide blank paper.

The Final Step in the Workshop: Sharing

Sharing time is the wrap-up for the day. Now you reconnect children to the minilesson, explore how the children tried the objective, and bring closure to the day's reading work. It's also a great time for reteaching, and I encourage you to grab this time and make it meaningful. It is, of course, always meaningful for children to share their thoughts and writing with peers, but when you guide them to teach *one another* about what they tried in the workshop, learning is more powerful.

During share time, the children gather on the floor in the meeting area. In order for share time to go smoothly, plan ahead. Have one or two children in mind whom you will call on to share their thinking and their reading responses. Pick children who have tried out what you taught in the minilesson, and then have them share their reading and explain their thinking aloud. Often, I pause after each child shares to recap what she said, relating the information back to the teaching chart from the minilesson. After the children I selected have shared, I extend an invitation to the whole class. This gives everyone an opportunity to participate. It is a good idea to keep track of who has shared so that you rotate and all the children have a chance to share over time.

What the Share Time Might Look Like
Lori calls the class back to the floor; she has turned on the tape recorder, and Beethoven's Fifth Symphony wafts around the room. The music is a signal to come to the floor. The children scurry around, cleaning up. They organize their books in the book boxes and return them to their places on the shelf. They put pencils and extra paper away. Slowly, the children begin to gather on the floor at Lori's feet. After a few minutes the children are settled on the carpet, their selected books and reading response papers neatly organized at their feet.

"OK, everyone," Lori says, "we had a great day in the workshop today. Many of us made several connections to the books we read, and I am so thrilled with how all of you wrote about your connections. I have one person in mind whom I would like to have launch our share time today. Samantha wrote about her connection, and she did a great job of telling exactly what happened in the book that reminded her of when she went to her mom's work. Samantha, are you ready to share?"

Samantha smiles and then studies her paper; she slowly reads her writing out loud to the class. "This is the page that reminded me of my connection," she says, opening her book to the page she picked out and showing the class the picture. "See how the mom is driving to work? The book says that she is going to work and misses her little girl. That reminded me of when I went to my mom's work."

Seven Essential Elements of Reading Workshop

As your vision of a reading workshop develops, remember three simple steps: present, demonstrate, coach. You will introduce a classroom strategy, show children how to practice the strategy during the workshop, and then coach them while they do so. Reading research points out seven essential elements that naturally become the focus during purposeful workshop instruction. These components maximize children's learning and accelerate their understanding of literacy, print, and what it means to be a reader (Pearson and Duke 2002):

- an *explicit description* of the reading or writing strategy
- *direct instruction* followed by guided practice
- teacher and student *modeling* of the strategy in real time
- *interactive* use of the strategy
- focus on a *gradual release of responsibility* for a strategy
- authentic *independent practice* for reading and writing strategies
- *immersion* in a print environment

CHAPTER FOUR

Creating a Literacy-Rich Environment

Now that you know what to do, you're ready to set up the workshop. How you arrange your classroom makes all the difference in the world. If the spaces flow together easily, the children will be able to move around the room during the workshop as needed. How you position the furniture has an impact on the independence students will exhibit in your classroom. Having a large number of books prominently displayed emphasizes the importance of print and encourages children to read. The other things you display in your classroom also send a message to children: the walls should teach for you. Think of those walls as a tool for tweaking and nurturing student thinking, rather than a place to display student work or pretty pictures.

Your classroom setup can support your instruction, your students' learning, and the overall management of your classroom community (Taberski 2000). There are three main things to pay attention to when setting up your classroom for reading workshop:

- the furniture arrangement
- the classroom library
- the classroom walls

Organize Your Classroom for Focused Literacy Instruction

Your room will need smooth transitions between your group meeting area, the students' desks, the classroom library, and the teaching areas along the perimeter. If your school allows you to replace desks with tables or to reduce the pieces of furniture in the room, your task will be easier. Unfortunately I have never had this luxury; I've always had to make the classroom work with what was there. But it can be done. You can create a workshop with any furniture available to you; the point is to give children a choice of work areas, time for purposeful practice, exposure to many, many books, and a lot of comfy places in the classroom to read.

Patti's third-grade Pinedale Elementary School classroom is an excellent example of how to set up a workshop. She has grouped individual desks together to create tables. She has brought in two bookshelves and a rug to make the reading and meeting area cozy and organized. She has rearranged the front of the room to accommodate her overhead projector and a small cart filled with the other materials she needs to teach her minilessons: craft sticks, whiteboards, dry-erase markers, and an assortment of pencils and sticky-note pads. Nearby she has chart paper and an assortment of pens to use during minilessons and teachable moments. Patti's room flows from the meeting area to the library to the students' desks to her teaching area.

Pam's second-grade classroom, which also provides excellent learning support, is set up a bit differently (see Figure 4.1). Pam has two teaching areas—a large kidney-shaped table, which she uses for guided reading and small-group math lessons, and a group meeting area. If another adult (a bilingual aide or a student teacher, for example) is working in the room, the areas can be used simultaneously. The group area is framed by bookshelves, a large chair, and an easel. Delineating it in this way gives the area a special focus and a cozy feeling. Pam's library faces the group meeting area, so that

FIGURE 4.1 Pam's Room Set Up For Reading Workshop

children can choose and return books without disturbing her guided reading instruction.

Pam has ample space on and around her teaching table for supplies. On the table is a basket filled with different-size sticky notes and pencils. Behind her she has a handy plastic bin, its drawers filled with dry-erase boards the size of index cards, 8½-by-11-inch dry-erase boards, dry-erase markers and erasers, sentence strips, markers, magnetic letters, and index cards of assorted sizes and varieties.

Student supplies can also be organized in tubs or other containers and placed on the floor near their desks for easy access (see the examples in Figures 4.2 and 4.3).

The Classroom Library and Other Books

The most important things in your classroom that will support your students' reading ability and development are books. Books need to be available in abundance and in a wide variety of genres. Children need to be exposed to many kinds of books, at all times, because children who are surrounded by books that they can pick up and browse through will read more and read widely, and children who read often tend to be better readers (Krashen 1997; IRA 2000).

Children living in poverty rarely have books in their homes. Unfortunately, they often don't have a chance to go to a library either. Your class-

FIGURE 4.2 Organize Student Materials for Easy Access

FIGURE 4.3

room library is their lifeline. It needs to support their curiosity about books and encourage a lifelong reading habit.

A library with two sections works best. Fill one section with picture books, simple stories and novels, nonfiction texts, biographies, magazines, poetry, and other kinds of print that appeal to the children in your class. In the other section place leveled texts that you can use to scaffold children's independent reading. It is important for children to be able to select their own "just right" texts (Taberski 2000). Providing lots of texts that students are able to read successfully on their own ensures that they are reading many, many words per year. The more words they read, the better readers they will become, the more their vocabularies will grow, and the more information they will know about the world (Krashen 1997, 2003).

The other important feature in your classroom is the print, picture books, and nonfiction materials that you display around the room. Your classroom needs to be rich with books and printed materials that are beautiful and pique student interest. Display books in every nook and cranny you can find, stack them in baskets, and place them on small folding easels. The number of books on display affects the atmosphere in your classroom: it puts literacy first. Figure 4.4 shows how Pam displays text in her room. Notice how inviting the books appear.

You don't have to spend a fortune to gather books for your classroom. Book clubs (Scholastic has several, at different levels) offer books at low prices, and you can also find books at discount shops and thrift stores. If you do want to spend more on a few hardcover picture books, choose books that will become old favorites you can return to again and again. Place books that are appealing to you and your students near your class meeting area so that they will be handy for modeling reading strategies during minilessons. Figure 4.5 shows class favorites from an author study organized so students can easily browse through them.

How Books Guide Children's Perception of Literacy

When children enter school for the first time, the knowledge they bring with them about books may not be very deep. Some may have never seen books in their home, and the adults they live with may not read any kind of text very often (if at all). Children's home experiences and their cultural background determine the literacy experiences they come to expect. In other words, if there are very few books in Maria's home, Maria won't *expect* books at school.

FIGURE 4.4 Display Books in Clever Ways to Pique Student Interest

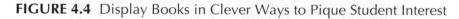

Chapter Four

FIGURE 4.5 Display Class Favorites Near the Group Meeting Area in an Inviting Way

Our classrooms are also a culture that children learn. The way we approach reading and writing, the way we use language, and how we use print all impress a culture of literacy on our students. Children's growth as readers and writers spirals. We need to build an atmosphere based on books and text so that children come to *expect* books to be available. We need to build an atmosphere that encourages reading and shows children that reading is a life-sustaining activity. When they leave our classroom, we want them to have developed a habit that they will carry with them through the upper grades.

If our classrooms are devoid of rich literature and instead are full of paper-and-pencil activities *about* reading, this is what our children will perceive reading to be. Likewise, if our classrooms are swimming in print and loaded with books and other media that children are invited to interact with daily, then children will develop a view of reading and writing as pleasurable and useful. We can accelerate children's literacy by creating text-rich environments that say, *Reading is important here.* High levels of literacy support can help children from low-socioeconomic-status homes or diverse cultural backgrounds accelerate their literacy learning (McGee and Richgels 2003; Snow, Burns, and Griffin 1998).

How Texts Support Children's Reading Growth

Children begin learning about literacy by becoming increasingly aware of how print works and of the alphabetic principle. Some children come to school with more understanding and experience than others, but all children learn along a continuum that increases their skills as they become readers (Adams 1990). As their learning spirals, the books in your library support and guide the children along this increasingly complex path (Clay 2001).This is especially important for children who seem to be struggling readers: they need lots and lots of opportunities to read.

Young proficient readers are developing effective self-monitoring and self-correcting strategies consistent with the texts they are reading, even though they are minimally aware of these strategies (Clay 2001). Young proficient readers focus on two processes: word processing, which includes letters and words, and sentence processing, which includes structure and meaning. Young struggling readers are not developing these systems effectively. They need help to develop this self-extending system.

Struggling readers need frequent experiences with books during the workshop because without lots and lots of practice, they fail to build the perceptual and cognitive strategies to make decisions as they work through texts. They are not able to pull together separate processing activities into smooth and integrated thoughts and meaning, and they don't develop efficient cognitive control mechanisms (or strategies) (Clay 2001). Your library must be filled with leveled texts to help young struggling readers grasp how to apply self-monitoring and self-correcting strategies. It must also be filled with texts that help young proficient readers develop the complex processing systems they have under way.

What Books Belong in the Classroom Library?

It is important to get a handle on how you are going to stock your classroom library, and with what. No teacher has unlimited resources, so you need to choose. You can begin your classroom library with a few books and add to the collection each year. Your classroom library needs three types of materials:

- leveled texts
- high-interest books
- references and multimedia resources

All three types of materials need to include both fiction and nonfiction. It is important to maintain a balance. After all, as adults, we read nonfiction, or informational texts, far more often than we read fiction.

Leveled Texts

Leveled texts are books designed for reading instruction and arranged along a gradient of difficulty (Fountas and Pinnell 2006). Irene C. Fountas and Gay Su Pinnell's text gradient ranges from level A through level Z, kindergarten through eighth grade. The Developmental Reading Assessment also has a text gradient (Beaver 2004). The primary DRA text gradient ranges from level 1 through level 38. For further information on text levels, see *Teaching for Comprehending and Fluency*, by Irene C. Fountas and Gay Su Pinnell (2006).

Leveled texts support the perceptual and cognitive strategies that children are developing. Specifically, leveled texts

- support the development of reading strategies
- give children the opportunity to practice selected strategies with selected text
- support independent reading by matching a text level with a child's ability level
- scaffold learning by controlling the text difficulty and text features

High-Interest Books

High-interest books are not specifically designed for reading instruction. They are picture books, poetry books, chapter books, and any other trade books that are meant to be read for pleasure or information. These books are not leveled. Your classroom library may organize high-interest books by theme, author, or subject. If your classroom library is short on these types of books, any anthologies full of good children's literature can be included.

Reference Books and Multimedia Resources

Your library also needs to include reference materials (dictionaries and how-to books, for example) and other sources of environmental print, like charts, posters, newspapers, magazines, catalogs, CDs, DVDs, and—ideally—an Internet connection. Many teachers include books related to the science and social study themes they teach over the course of a year.

What a Classroom Library May Look Like

An assortment of books will support and entice young readers. Figure 4.6 is a picture of Hollie's classroom library. She has baskets of nonfiction and fiction books. She also has sets of leveled texts divided into three general (color-coded) categories—high, medium, and easy. It is important to give children options when they choose books from the leveled book baskets. They should not be limited to a narrow text level but rather given a range of books from which they can choose the one that is just right.

Hollie both color-codes and assigns numbers to her leveled-book baskets—red 1, red 2, red 3; green 1, green 2, green 3; and blue 1, blue 2, blue 3 (see Figure 4.7). Red books are slightly easier than green books, which are slightly easier than blue books. Red 1 books are slightly easier than red 2 books, and so on. In this quick way, Hollie organizes nine categories that span several Fountas and Pinnell or DRA levels. Choosing a book on their own from one of the levels, children are assured of getting a just-right book, are still able to choose books independently, and learn to use the library with confidence.

A library for younger readers would look somewhat different. Kristina's first-grade classroom doesn't have as many bookcases, so she

FIGURE 4.6 Hollie's Classroom Library

FIGURE 4.7 Hollie's Book Baskets Organized by General Levels

FIGURE 4.8 A First-Grade Library

organizes her books in baskets and places them, low to the floor, around the room (see Figure 4.8). The children select their books when they enter the classroom for the day, during a routine Kristina calls "book switch," just before reading workshop. Kristina doesn't want the children wandering around the room when they should be getting a lot of reading done! (Chapters 9 and 10 provide more information on setting up effective libraries in kindergarten and first grade, respectively.)

Time to Begin Teaching

You're ready to begin. Your room is set up, your library organized, the book boxes labeled, and it is time to start *doing*—to teach in this beautiful environment, the air full of expectancy and hope. In launching a reading workshop, you are setting in motion a conceptual development program focused on skills. Children will learn to read through authentic and purposeful literacy activities that spiral learning and tailor instruction to their needs.

Yes, your expertise will grow and you will be able to respond to each child's developmental needs with more precision over time, but don't worry, you will be successful right away. The National Reading Panel report points out that teachers who continue to develop effective new teaching strategies are more apt to control their own instructional decisions and, in turn, affect student learning (NICHD 2000). When you learn new teaching strategies and methods with the intention of increasing student learning, you are taking a whole lot of steps in the right direction.

Your students will learn as you learn to create a cohesive, focused workshop, even when your instruction isn't perfect. Improving your practice and implementing what you have learned will lead to greater student achievement. So go ahead. Launch a focused workshop, reflect on your mistakes along the way, and then seek out more information on reading instruction to help you improve. All you have to gain is to become a more expert teacher.

CHAPTER FIVE

Units of Study

What to Teach

"**W**e are going to begin planning your reading workshop by mapping out minilessons," I said to a small group of teachers at a recent staff development session I was conducting. "First, I need you to suspend judgment for a moment and trust yourselves. I am going to ask you to think deeply about how to teach reading in your room. Thinking like this feels like a journey, an important one, but it is new because you won't be following a teachers' manual. Are you ready?"

A team of four first-grade teachers to my right were still considering what I had said. They didn't respond.

"I don't know all the answers, because I don't know your students very well," I continued, "but you do. And I can help you think of how to plan curriculum. By the end of the day you will have clear direction for teaching the first few weeks of a reading workshop."

A team of three second-grade teachers in the middle of the room talked among themselves for a moment. Then one of them, Sarah, raised her hand. "It feels confusing right now. I've seen the children at work in your classrooms at Pinedale, so I have *seen* what I need to do, but I don't know how to do it."

"Great! Then we have a place to start. We can *see* in our minds what we need to teach, and how we want our classrooms to flow and feel, but we don't *know how* to roll out the curriculum to get there. Am I close to your thinking about what you need right now?"

There was a collective sigh in the room, almost as if the air had changed, been made lighter by the revelation. It was important for this group of teachers to admit they didn't know how to plan instruction for a reading workshop. It was important for me to admit that I didn't have all the answers. It was important for us to work together so that they could feel confident they were moving in the right direction. All the teachers had previously taught using a reading program that came with a teachers' manual, each month planned out. The manual had told them what they needed to do each day. But these teachers didn't think the program met the needs of all their students. They *wanted* to try something new but felt paralyzed to do it on their own. They wanted a clear direction: specifically, they wanted to know what to do during the first lessons in a reading workshop.

Organizing workshop instruction for the first time takes tremendous energy. Just setting up the room and preparing it for reading workshop is time-consuming. It is natural to want a guidebook to tell you what to do. Launching the first few lessons can be even more daunting: teaching in a new way means taking risks, and taking risks always feels uncomfortable.

If you are new to workshop teaching, rest assured that you are on the right track. Just begin slowly with one unit of study, and keep your focus on that. Your goal is to move the children forward along the literacy continuum, one step at a time, while accelerating their growth and maximizing your instruction by using the structures and routines discussed in previous chapters. These include

- organizing your classroom to facilitate reading workshop with focused minilessons
- time spent reading
- time spent writing about reading
- meeting with small groups for reading instruction
- conferring with children one-on-one

Why Change Is Important

Workshop instruction can be very powerful for ethnically diverse and poor children. The current push in public education is for our children to learn *more* than they have learned in the past and to *achieve* at higher levels as measured by scores on standardized tests. While this can be frustrating, remember that for many years the children traditionally served in schools that received Title I money had not achieved at the same levels or rates as children from higher socioeconomic backgrounds. Because of this history and the pressure of being held accountable for test scores, many teachers feel obligated to teach only from a textbook in a traditional way—a way that requires children to spend large amounts of time filling in worksheets or parroting answers to teacher questions. Fear of accountability pushes us to consider this type of instruction; after all, our students' performance on standardized tests will be used as the sole measure of our schools' and our teaching performance. Ironically, research *does not* support this type of teaching.

In fact, research reported by the National Reading Panel states clearly that the best practices for maximizing learning and helping students comprehend text include the following (NICHD 2000):

- thoroughly explaining what is taught—*what* to do, *how* to do it, *when*, and *why*
- incorporating reading activities and teaching strategies that demand *active engagement*
- Asking questions of the text and discussing possible answers
- modeling thinking processes for students

When workshops provide focused instruction, they can lead to higher student achievement. This focused instruction begins with your minilesson. You need to teach to one objective in the minilesson and model what you want the children to work on during the workshop. It is important that they are engaged and focused. For too many years, children had to learn skills by rote in traditional lessons that were boring and that did not actively engage them. Then, the pendulum swung the other way, and for too many years our instruction provided too much freedom; children were invited to participate in workshops but not expected to practice the strategies and skills we were teaching. Neither approach is acceptable if you want all students to excel.

When you focus your instruction with precise minilessons, children have the opportunity to hear you describe a strategy, watch you model it, and then practice the same strategy during the workshop. If a student re-sists trying the strategy, I redirect him: I tell him to focus on what I have taught, modeled, and practiced for the class so he can do the same thing while I coach and guide him. The children I work with don't have anyone outside school to support their literacy development; I need them to make the best use of their time in school and their time with me.

Organizing the Workshop Curriculum Around Units of Study

The reading workshop curriculum is organized into units of study. A unit of study is a group of lessons, developed around a theme or reading com-prehension strategy, that roll out in a sequential and purposeful manner. Each unit lasts four to five weeks and focuses on improving children's read-ing ability. *Everything* in the workshop is about helping children become better readers. Over the course of a year you will teach between eight and ten units. Each unit will contain twenty to twenty-five minilessons. These units should be tied to your state standards or curriculum expectations and should incorporate the components of all good reading instruction programs, including (Akhavan 2004):

- phonics
- fluency
- comprehension

The expectations for each unit of study build on what has been learned in previous units, so as the curriculum rolls out, the children are deepening and extending their word recognition skills and the cognitive processing skills that help them become fluent readers. The minilessons and student work in your units incorporate both these skill categories. You teach skills and strategies during the minilesson; the children then practice these skills and strategies independently during the remainder of the workshop.

Planning Units of Study

Units of study provide a comprehensive learning opportunity for at-risk learners and accelerate their learning so that they are able to catch up with their non-at-risk peers (Akhavan 2006). This acceleration is possible when the unit focuses on a particular theme or reading comprehension strategy and is organized in a logical, purposeful manner. Specifically, this means that the lessons are explicit, practice time is built into the workshop, each lesson is based on what research says works for children who need support, and there is little downtime for learners and their teachers. Each unit

- sets a purpose for instruction
- organizes instruction based on student assessment
- defines what students will do during the workshop
- includes direct instruction by the teacher
- provides cooperative learning opportunities for children

The unit of study is an overall guide. It provides the theme for and drives the purpose of each minilesson, the work students do during the workshop, the written response, and the wrap-up or sharing that occurs at the end of the workshop. (See Chapter 3 for more on these components of the reading workshop.) This theme enables you to stay on track and help at-risk learners accelerate their literacy progress. As you build on the strategies or lessons from previous units, children constantly practice their acquired skills. This continuing practice helps them become independent and successful readers. For examples of complete units of study, see Chapters 9 through 11.

Support Units of Study with Research-Based Teaching

Teach what works based on the research. If you are working with an at-risk population of children, focus your teaching on what the research says works for these children in particular. Studies clearly point out what works in literacy instruction for young children: while they do need explicit instruction in decoding and the alphabetic principle, and do need to practice reading fluently, these important skills are not everything they need to become effective readers (Smolkin and Donovan 2002). For example, instruction in decoding does not necessarily build vocabulary or general knowledge; these are better developed by *reading text* (Nagy and Scott 2000). Young children also need instruction in *comprehension*, beginning in the very early grades (Block and Pressley 2003; Pearson and Duke 2002; Smolkin and Donovan 2002; Williams 2002). While *decoding* instruction focuses on teaching the associational skills of attaching phonemes to letters, *comprehension* instruction focuses on deductive and interpretive skills. Young children have trouble thinking multidimensionally and develop their interpretive skills over time. They need to be exposed to comprehension strategy instruction that is interactive and modeled frequently (Liang and Dole 2006; Smolkin and Donovan 2002).

Several studies suggest that effective primary-grade teachers of high-poverty populations or at-risk children focus on the systematic and explicit teaching of comprehension strategies *in combination with* a phonics program and the teaching of high-frequency words. These studies show that highly effective teachers do three things:

- coach children on word recognition strategies (fix-up strategies) and comprehension strategies during the actual reading of texts
- emphasize higher-order comprehension questions and discussion
- provide numerous opportunities for children to write in response to their reading (Adams 1990; Allington and Cunningham 1999; NICHD 2000; Patterson et al. 2003; Pearson and Duke 2002; Snow et al. 1998; Taylor et al. 1999; Taylor, Pearson, et al. 2002; Taylor, Peterson, et al. 2002; Wharton-McDonald et al. 1998)

Overall, the focus on higher-order comprehension questions and discussion is not for children to get the right answer but rather to use the texts to support and justify their answers (Pearson and Duke 2002).

The National Reading Panel recognizes that learning to read involves two basic processes. One, word recognition, involves learning to convert letters into words; the other involves comprehending the meaning of the print. Word recognition skills are taught during the literacy block (discussed in Chapter 2) and are reinforced in guided reading lessons during reading workshop. Comprehension strategies are taught in the minilessons that begin each day's reading workshop and are also reinforced during guided reading.

How to Approach Comprehension Instruction

Research reviewed by the National Reading Panel (NICHD 2000) suggests that direct instruction of comprehension strategies is a way to break through children's passive approach to learning and help them actively focus on reading and how they think while reading. The panel recommended seven categories of comprehension strategy instruction:

- actively monitoring comprehension
- incorporating cooperative learning
- using graphic and semantic organizers
- focusing on answering questions

- focusing on asking questions
- identifying story structure
- summarizing

The research also identified an eighth category, *using multiple strategies*, in which teachers and students read a text interactively, with the teacher modeling how to approach a text using two or more strategies (often combining several of the above categories) to make meaning.

Other research points to a broader number of comprehension strategies that aid children in learning to read. These include mental imagery and mnemonic strategies, active listening, prior knowledge, prediction, and thinking aloud (Block and Pressley 2003; Pearson and Duke 2002).

Figure 5.1 lists a few reading comprehension strategies along with its purpose and outcome to help you visualize how these strategies apply to your daily classroom instruction.

How to Teach Comprehension Effectively

Researchers have reviewed numerous studies and identified effective ways to teach comprehension strategies. Effective comprehension instruction includes

- explicitly teaching a comprehension strategy
- talking about it clearly with children
- modeling when and how to apply it during reading

These procedures include teachers thinking aloud about their own use of the strategy and giving children time to discuss with classmates how using the strategy helped them understand the text (Afflerbach 2002; Baker 2002; Block and Israel 2004; Diehl 2005; Pardo 2004; Pearson and Duke 2002; Trabasso and Bouchard 2002).

Incorporating Effective Teaching Strategies into Reading Workshop

Research-based teaching strategies fit into the workshop in two ways. The first is through the structure of the workshop, with its focus on transactional teaching. Second, some research-based strategies become the themes, or overarching ideas, of the workshop's units of study; they glue the mini-lessons together.

Strategies Inherent to Workshop Structure

Several research-based strategies are *part* of what we do every day in the workshop but don't qualify as overarching themes. These strategies include

- mnemonic devices
- graphic organizers
- cooperative learning

FIGURE 5.1 Reading Comprehension Strategies and Outcomes

Strategic Teaching for Supporting Reading		Strategic Teaching for Extending Thinking	
Unit Focus	**Procedures Taught and Practiced**	**Unit Focus**	**Procedures Taught and Practiced**
Decoding Words	Converting letters into sounds and blending them to form words	Predicting	Making predictions and drawing conclusions; using reading response sheet
Solving Words/Analog	Remembering words already known and using word parts to read new word (If I know -ought in bought, I know sought.)	Text Connnections	Making connections between what is read and personal experiences, connections to other texts and media, and connections to world events, facts, and general knowledge
Monitoring	Checking that the reading sounds right, looks right, and makes sense	Inferring	Understanding that texts do not state all facts, but that some knowledge and meaning is deducted from events and facts in the text
Using Information in Text/Predicting	Using context clues, linguistic and background knowledge, and memory to anticipate unknown words	Synthesizing Text	Combining information from the text with the reader's background knowledge to create new under-standing and conceptual development
Searching for Sight Words	Retrieving words already learned from memory	Retelling	Remembering the events in a story in proper sequence, including story elements and major events affecting the plot
Fluency	Integrating cognitive skills that result in smooth, flowing, expressive reading	Mental Imagery	Using background knowledge to envision what is read
Summarizing	Remembering important information and disregarding irrelevant details	Questioning	Formulating and answering questions of the text or of the author while reading to enhance comprehension
		Story Elements	Learning the parts of narrative text structure; analyzing texts based on these elements
		Informational Text Structure	Learning the structure of non-fiction texts; using this structure to understand the information given
		Clarifying and Monitoring Comprehension	Checking for understanding by thinking aloud or to oneself about what has occurred in a story, or about the facts given in a nonfiction book

Each component of the workshop relies on these research-based strategies to help children become fluent readers. Remember, reading develops best through activities that focus on the purpose and function of reading and writing—allowing children to work together, visualize information, and use cues to wake up their brains (NICHD 2000).

Mnemonic devices and think-alouds
The minilesson is a short, power-packed lesson. The power derives from

- activating prior knowledge
- telling children what they need to know
- reinforcing learning by repeating a few key phrases
- modeling your thinking
- adding to a teaching chart that records learning and thinking

The minilesson is a grand opportunity to provide a mnemonic device to help children remember information. Any pictorial aid you create, show, use, and think through helps children remember information and comprehend text. The perfect pictorial aid is the teaching chart. It is best to create, or at least add to, the chart during the lesson, in conjunction with your students. This adds context to everything you say. It also creates a record of thinking and learning that you can use on your walls. Remember, you want your classroom to be filled with purposeful print that children can refer to when working independently.

When you combine the teaching chart with a few key phrases you repeat often, *and even record on the chart*, you help the young readers in your room improve their memory. You might have favorite phrases for each unit. For example, in the unit on making connections, I use specific vocabulary with children like *my text connection*. During a unit on imagery I tell children I see *a movie in my mind*. These key words and phrases are powerful learning strategies for young children. Thinking through these strategies aloud, you unveil your thought processes for children, making them transparent. Children learn to think, step-by-step, as you discuss the strategy aloud while you model it.

Graphic organizers
Your graphic organizers should mirror and reinforce the focus of the unit of study. The teaching chart described earlier is really just a big graphic organizer. It helps children see information in new ways, records your thinking in a different form, and gives you the opportunity to show children *how* to use graphic organizers when composing a reading response. Graphic organizers are visuals with *purpose*; they are not busywork.

As I mentioned in Chapter 3, special paper for reader responses can be designed as graphic organizers and can help scaffold children's thinking as they write about the books they've read. When children write about their reading, they

- use metacognitive strategies—they think about their thinking
- record their thinking
- organize their thinking and refine their comprehension of texts
- use an organizational aid to help them remember meaning

There is no one right way or wrong way to create a graphic organizer to guide student reading response. Whatever organizer you use, you should demonstrate how to use it on your teaching chart; the children can then use their own identical organizer when writing about their reading. I find it helpful to keep these reading response sheets in a folder so that you have a record of each child's progress. Copies of these graphic organizers are included in the appendix.

Graphic organizers help children stay organized, which helps them attend to the task at hand. Writing on an organizer also helps them learn and internalize the structure of the reading comprehension strategy.

Sometimes you may want to stretch the written response options you normally provide in the workshop (and the paper you design for them). See Chapter 3 for a deeper discussion.

Cooperative learning
The focused and sustained nature of reading workshop fosters thinking because you are

- giving children time to practice sustained reading
- giving children time to share their thoughts about reading with a partner
- allowing children to help each other figure out unknown words independently while you meet with guided reading groups
- allowing children to practice together what you have demonstrated in the minilesson

Cooperative learning is an integral part of the workshop. During the workshop, children meet with partners to practice reading aloud, clarify understanding of texts, share tidbits of information from books, share their writing about reading, and help each other figure out words. Children often learn as much from each other as they do from us. By sharing information and strategies with each other, they learn to focus on and discuss reading comprehension and fix-up strategies. Often, I see children who are working together grinning with the elation of helping someone else.

Comprehension Strategies That Guide Units of Study
Teaching manuals and professional articles and books list multiple comprehension strategies that are effective for increasing children's ability to read. The following eight strategies, when combined, can constitute a yearlong curriculum. The minilessons and reading responses of each four- or five-week unit of study would focus on one strategy, building on what has been learned in previous units.

Reading comprehension strategies that I recommend for primary classrooms include the following (Pearson and Duke 2002; Tracey and Morrow 2002):

- making text connections
- retelling
- creating mental images, or visualizing
- making predictions and drawing conclusions
- questioning
- summarizing
- identifying story elements
- identifying informational text structures
- clarifying and monitoring comprehension, or thinking aloud

If you teach very young children, you may want to focus on fewer strategies. For example, in kindergarten you may choose to focus on retelling, text connections, and imagery. By the same token, if you are teaching second or third grade, you will want your strategy instruction to be deeper and more complex than the instruction your students received in earlier grades.

But be careful; it is easy to overfocus on the strategy and forget that the goal is for children to make meaning while reading (Duffy 2002; Liang and Dole 2006; Sinatra et al. 2002). Specific reading strategies can provide a theme for a unit of study, but the overall focus should always be on children *applying* the strategy while reading. This keeps children focused on meaning, while the act of reading simultaneously builds background knowledge, develops vocabulary, and increases fluency.

Our goal is to help children become active participants who construct meaning through intentional problem solving. We want their thinking to be influenced by the text and by their prior knowledge (Trabasso and Bouchard 2002; Tracey and Morrow 2002). We want them to be aware of the strategy they are applying.

The Unit of Study

As I've said, each unit is based on a particular reading strategy or fix-up strategy and is titled to reflect the focus of the work children will produce during the unit. For example, during a unit on summarizing, children will write summaries of the text; during a unit on visualization, children will draw pictures and describe what they see in their minds.

The Minilesson

The reading workshop in first, second, and third grades begins with a minilesson dealing with some component of the comprehension strategy to which the unit of study is devoted. In the lesson, you explain what the skill or technique is and how it is useful. You then model the procedure, writing down key components on a teaching chart and giving students an opportunity to use it before going off to work in the workshop. Your focus is on thinking aloud as you demonstrate the strategy and show children how they can use the strategy on their own. During this demonstration you focus on higher-order questions about the text and emphasize how the children will write in response to their reading during the workshop.

After the minilesson, the children go off to work independently while you either conduct one-on-one conferences or meet with guided reading groups. Again, you'll explicitly coach students in the use of the skill, technique, or procedure as appropriate for the group or individual.

The Interactive Read-Aloud in Kindergarten

One way to guide a kindergarten reading workshop is through an interactive read-aloud. The daily schedule in Chapter 2 presents the read-aloud as a literacy block component separate from the reading workshop. This is the preferred approach. However, if you have very little wiggle room in your daily schedule, the interactive read-aloud is an effective way to run a reading workshop with young children. Pearson and Duke (2002) found that kindergartners improve their comprehension of books read aloud by focusing explicitly on a comprehension strategy for an extended length of time.

Begin with a short discussion about what the focus of the interactive read-aloud will be. Then read a picture book aloud, stopping to model your thinking and your use of the focus comprehension strategy aloud, prompt a discussion about the text and the strategy, and draw the children's attention to text features. After the interactive read-aloud, the children, with a partner or in small groups, discuss the story in relation to the focus strategy before moving on to write an individual response. Both the oral and the written reading responses should focus on the strategy being taught. For example, if the strategy is retelling, the children would meet with a partner (or with you in a guided group) and retell the story. Then the children can individually draw a picture or write a few sentences to retell the story.

Always Teach, Teach, Teach

Workshop instruction is focused teaching—teaching you are in charge of. Any classroom structure, progressive or traditional, that allows children to meander aimlessly through the school year, gleaning only *some* information, is not effective. The best instruction guides children to an exact understanding of what should be taught. Durkin (1978–79) points out that when we "mention" something to kids we are not teaching. I agree. Mentioning (or assigning, for that matter) is not teaching. When you focus your workshop with a research-based unit of study, you are *teaching* and, more important, you are working to close the achievement gap that so many young children face each day in school.

Teaching means we are

- showing
- directing
- modeling
- highlighting

- guiding
- informing
- re-forming
- thinking aloud

CHAPTER SIX

The Strategy Backpack
Focusing on Student Learning by Teaching Strategies

The children arrive at my school each day expectant. Their backpack shoulder straps are neat and snug, their hair is combed just so, and Mom's, Dad's, or Grandma's kiss has left a faint wet spot on their forehead. They arrive each day ready for school. Each child brings his or her wonder, expectation, and desire to learn. Each also brings a large dose of uncertainty to the classroom.

The children in Pinedale's kindergarten through third-grade classrooms are eager, trusting, and innocent. They know that there is much to grasp, that they have to listen, and that they are expected to "do their job" at school: to read their books during reading time and write lots and lots during writing time. We tell them to think and explore, and we tell them they are smart—very smart.

And they believe us.

Our job, then, is to focus on them and help them succeed.

There are many factors in every child's life that will impact how much we are able to do with and for the children that arrive at our classroom doors each morning. But one important thing we can do is *fill their strategy backpacks*. I want each child in my school to be an independent reader and writer. I want them all to read and comprehend. I want them to write with fluency and enjoyment. They will not come by the ability to do these things by accident.

Teachers must focus on what the children need to know and be able to do and then teach children *how* to do these things. Effective strategy instruction keeps its focus on kids. This focus conveys to children that

- they are important
- you will be there for them as they learn

- together they will learn what they need to know and be able to do
- they need to practice real reading and writing, not waste time doing *stuff*

What Is a Strategy Backpack?

Visualize a backpack strapped to the back of each child entering your classroom. One by one they file in, a small, invisible backpack attached to each little body. Some already have strategies in their backpack, things they can do on their own that enable them to read and write successfully. Others may not have anything in their backpack at all. It doesn't matter. Your job is to fill up the backpack and reinforce whatever is already there.

Reading-strategy backpacks are filled with fix-up strategies and comprehension strategies like those discussed in the previous chapter—strategies that help each child figure out unknown words and understand what he has read. Writing-strategy backpacks are filled with an acquired understanding of story, the ability to focus on an important moment in time, the ability to hear sounds in words and write those sounds down, and the knowledge of how to share all this with a friend. Children's strategy backpacks fill up throughout the year with the skills and knowledge that help them succeed at reading and writing at their grade level.

Fostering Independence

One day I listened to Lela read in Gloria Alvarez's second-grade classroom. Lela was intent and confident. She would read and then glance up at me with a wide smile. While I listened to Lela, I looked through Gloria's anecdotal notes that were nearby on the teaching table. Gloria had taken a running record of Lela's reading. She noted that Lela's fluency was developing: she miscued on two words and overlooked only one period, and she inflected her voice at the appropriate places. As I listened to Lela read *Mr. Bumblesticker Goes to the Zoo* (Iverson 2000), I could tell that Lela loved the story. Afterward, she launched into a detailed retelling about Mr. and Mrs. Bumblesticker and how Mr. Bumblesticker was tricked by the seals. Lela had many strategies in her backpack to read this level J book as proficiently as she did. The strategies Lela had learned included

- getting her mouth ready for the first sound in the word
- looking at the pictures to figure out unknown text
- rereading

Gloria and I discussed possible next steps for Lela, as we didn't want her newfound reading wings to collapse. We chose a goal for her: *focus on chunking your words when you see a word you don't know*. We picked this goal because Lela didn't attempt chunking when she came to a word she didn't know; she just waited until one of us rushed in to save her by telling her the word. The next strategy she needed to develop was the ability to chunk and figure out unfamiliar words on her own. We wrote it on a sticky note and put it in her notebook so that she would be reminded of her new goal and the strategy she needed to focus on.

It is best when our students learn new strategies and skills with us sitting nearby, modeling, coaching, and encouraging. Then, when they succeed and reach the bar we have set for them, we can step in and raise the bar just a little bit higher; this is how we fill up students' strategy backpacks—a little bit at a time.

Lela was independent at level L, but not all of her classmates were fluent at this level. Some of the children were reading level D books. They were developing strategies that Lela had down pat.

Sometimes we feel validated when young children need us. They may wait for us at every step because they have a strong desire to get it right. It *is* our job to teach children how, to show them how. But eventually, the proof of our success as teachers is in what kids can do *alone*. Our goal is for them to succeed when we are not nearby, coaching over their shoulders.

Strategy backpacks are filled with skills, knowledge, and strategies that make kids independent. This independence comes step-by-step, as it did with Lela. At each level, at each step in their learning continuum, children move from dependency on us, their teachers, to a place of independence where they no longer need us to hold their hand—at least not at the same level or with the same writing expectation. We continually scaffold their learning so that as they become more independent, we move them forward to new learning, stretching them just a tad more. In this way, we move children from their current understanding and skills to the next level, where they then acquire a new set of skills and further understanding.

Scaffolded instruction

■ links prior knowledge to new learning
■ links ideas, skills, and developing competencies to skills and strategies already in place
■ determines students' current level of understanding and builds on it
■ provides supports (scaffolds) and gradually removes them as students demonstrate proficiency
■ focuses on Vygotsky's (1980) zone of proximal development

Vygotsky's Zone of Proximal Development

Vygotsky developed a social theory of learning that describes how we learn throughout our lives. The best predictor of what a child will learn at any given time is what that child already knows. Learning occurs when new concepts are *linked* to prior knowledge.

Vygotsky's theory of a zone of proximal development suggests that learning occurs when a teacher matches new information to a child's current level of understanding and then guides the child to learn the new material (Mazzoni and Gambrell 2003). A child's zone of proximal development is located just slightly above the child's current level of knowledge or understanding. The zone stretches from the child's current level of competence to a place where the child is able to learn with the help of a teacher or mentor (Darling-Hammond 1997). This is the level at which children learn best. If you reach *beyond* the child's zone of proximal development, you will find what some have called the child's zone of frustrational development (Baker, Hackett, and Wilhelm 2001) and it is time to take a step back.

Accelerating Student Learning

We have the power to accelerate student learning. This is a big responsibility. You may not believe it, but the future of your students is in your hands. Helping young children who live in poverty do as well in school as their higher-socioeconomic peers is truly a mission (Hale 2004).

You can accelerate learning by giving children your time and attention with heavy doses of explicit, purposeful instruction. Yes, *accelerate*. Accelerating learning is not a negative idea. It just means that you push children to learn and achieve at a fairly rapid pace. Young children who have to catch up need extra help. Consider all the information, ideas, and strategies they need to acquire to do as well as their more privileged peers. You have no choice but to focus and accelerate.

In order to teach well, we also have to keep children motivated. Young children come to us full of wonder and the desire to learn. Sometimes by third grade, the wonder and desire wane. I have sat in many meetings at which a special team discussed a child's progress in second or third grade and we noted that the child was no longer as motivated as other children, didn't complete homework, didn't read or write during the workshops, and in general didn't engage with the teacher or her own learning. This child has checked out emotionally. If a child has been struggling for three years, why would she keep trying in third grade?

Learning is an emotional journey. To be successful, a child has to believe he can accomplish the work before him and do it well. This means teaching the child in his zone of proximal development and respecting where that zone is. We cannot afford to burn children out at this tender age. It also means creating a classroom environment in which it is safe to take risks.

Creating Emotional Safety Nets

Students will take risks when we believe in them and when they know that their attempts to learn will not engender embarrassment or humiliation. What kid will take a risk if she knows she might become an "example" for the class? Not the students I've worked with! I admit there have been times that I have highlighted a student's mistake, thinking I was turning the mistake into a teachable moment. Each time, I knew midsentence that *I* had made a mistake. Even though I thought I was being kind and gentle, I could see in the eyes of the student a look that said, "Why are you embarrassing me? I cannot believe my teacher is making a big deal of this!" When working with very young children, kindergartners, for example, I have gotten the same look, although it often plays out a bit differently. They usually look down and start picking at their shoe or look at the ceiling, hoping for a way out.

My effort to avoid highlighting mistakes as teachable moments led me to think about a classroom environment that fosters taking risks. I want students to think, converse, and use new words in their conversations and writing, so I make a point to applaud kids for trying even if they miss the mark. A transactional model of instruction (in which students transact and interact with information in lessons) is key in encouraging them to take risks. The alternative, a transmission model of instruction (in which children passively receive information), does not provide students with opportunities to practice what they are supposed to be learning.

Transactional teaching helps foster safety nets in our classroom by giving children

- opportunities to practice reading strategies without judgment
- support and acceptance regarding their thinking about books and their word use
- authentic opportunities to use new vocabulary
- opportunities to participate in group and partner discussions
- opportunities to write about reading

To develop student learning and independence, we need to focus on filling their strategy backpacks; to keep the emotional environment in the classroom safe, we need to engage children in purposeful work and let them take risks without fear of embarrassment.

Discovering the Energy of Engagement

Energy and passion come from knowing. When children *know* things of value and sustenance, they *feel successful*. From the moment a child discovers he *knows* how to do something or understands what he has been studying and can explain it, he shines with the joy of success. This is the energy that creates motivated kids. Motivated children read. They write. They pay attention to what we show them, what we value in the classroom. And they work hard. Motivated children are successful at school.

But what about the kids who are not successful? No one wants to fail, and children who have grown accustomed to failure put up defense mechanisms. Sometimes they refuse to try, sometimes they don't pay attention, and sometimes they throw distractions our way. Mostly, they are just tired of failing.

Focus on accelerating reading and writing ability by giving children all the mental tools they need to be successful, to get it. Provide children with opportunities to learn that are within their personal zones of proximal development so that they can experience success and move forward from there.

What Is Explicit and Purposeful Instruction?

In well-designed workshops, *explicit* and *purposeful* complement each other perfectly. Explicit teaching is instruction that *shows* children something new, instruction that models and moves children to a level where they can function independently. Purposeful instruction flows from the teacher; it gently takes hold of a child's mind and says, *Look here, let me show you how*. To do this, you need to move from *assigning* to *teaching*.

Don't focus on the worksheet or skill, but on the child and the strategies that child is acquiring. Focus on the knowledge that child is gathering. To do this, you have to make your instruction and thinking transparent: you have to discuss your thinking, model, share, and show children how to read and write. You don't just assign and explain. You become a reader and a writer in front of your students each day during the minilesson. Lucy Calkins and Shelley Harwayne stated in their early work *The Writing Workshop: A World of Difference* (1987) that effective methods of teaching are transparent. In other words, when watching someone teach *explicitly*, you notice *how* she discusses books, *how* she chunks words, or *how* she wrestles with an idea in writing. You don't notice a stilted delivery or someone talking *about* something rather than *doing* something.

Instruction Should Foster Independence

How our students read and write when we aren't standing right beside them reveals what processes, or strategies, they have acquired. What they can do with us coaching them is equally important, but our goal is to move children to independence. We should focus on the work they do *without* us. To move students to this point, we need to create environments and provide instruction that move children from their current state of not knowing, or not knowing how, to a state where they can easily use a strategy, approach, or technique to read or write at an expected level in a particular genre. This becomes our modus operandi.

I see this idea as a stone that many of us trip over. When we invest our hearts in children, and pour hours and hours into teaching them well, sometimes we become convinced that they can do something on their own. But then, when we assess them, we realize that they cannot read or write as well on their own as we had thought. Then we feel a bit of disappointment; sometimes, we may even feel inadequate. We may try to reason away the apparent results—"Oh, Marco had a bad day, I know he knows it," or "Pang could read at that book level last week!"

This happens to everyone. As teachers we enjoy working with our students, we enjoying guiding them through a book or coaching their writing. We are focused on the work they do *with* us. But this is sometimes the wrong focus. We may feel that this is when we are doing our best work, but if we cannot move children to do on their own what they can do when they work with us, we have missed the target. Children need to leave our classroom proficient at the goals and objectives we set for them in reading and writing. It is best to think of these goals and objectives as benchmarks.

The benchmarks we set are road markers, giving us an indication of what children can do. Benchmarks should provide

- a mental picture of how to move students toward independence
- specific goals for increasing student reading ability
- a performance standard or expectation

Guided Instruction

Guided instruction is part of the release-of-responsibility model. It is our job continually to enlarge children's potential and their capacity to learn. While guiding children through one stage, we are conceptualizing the next piece, idea, or strategy they need to learn and own. We guide and release them through our instruction, but then we move on to something new and more difficult for which they need coaching. It is like a wheel. We're always directing our instruction toward the next possibility, and the children continually learn. We are never really done.

Think of guided instruction as moving along a continuum. At the beginning stages of literacy, children are not yet ready for guided reading. They work on prereading skills—developing concepts of print, listening to lots of books read to them aloud, and playing with words and letters. Later, they receive guided reading instruction targeted to their emerging conceptual development and practice reading a lot and often. On the left side of the continuum the teacher is highly involved with the children's reading behavior and bears much of the responsibility for literacy development. The children are mostly taking it in. As children take steps on their own, the teacher's responsibility diminishes. Perhaps the children move to reading chapter books and meeting with literature groups. However, they still need guidance and coaching in order to apply fix-up and comprehension strategies to more difficult texts. On the right side of the continuum the children are responsible for their learning and the teacher's involvement is less direct.

Figure 6.1 shows the release of responsibility occurring through different types of instruction. As the children develop reading abilities, your instruction responds to their needs and changes in general stages:

- pre–guided reading
- guided reading

- transitional guided reading
- guided literature groups
- literature groups

Transitional guided reading and guided literature groups are a bridge between guided reading and independent literature groups (Saunders-Smith 2002). Children need different kinds of coaching when reading books at higher levels of a text gradient. In transitional guided reading, children are reading more difficult texts (level M, N, or O books, for example), and you help them by breaking longer texts into parts, giving them a purpose for reading, and focusing on reading comprehension strategies. At the guided reading table, you help them make the transition from guided reading with heavy coaching to reading with intermittent coaching. They gradually develop from readers who are more dependent on direct teacher coaching into readers who self-monitor and self-coach while reading. Children often are not ready to function effectively in literature groups without teacher guidance. In guided literature groups, you coach children to think about texts and discuss texts in depth. Often, children need the guidance of a teacher facilitating the group before they are ready to launch a literature group independently.

As you provide expert guided instruction, it is important to know and understand what your students are expected to know and understand at each grade level. You can look at the relevant professional standards or at other state-adopted guidelines.

We guide and teach through explicit instruction in which we show children *how*, then provide guided help during our workshops. Three teaching opportunities occur during the workshop: the minilesson, guided reading, and conferring.

Minilessons Are Teaching Moments

As your students take control of a strategy, you move to the next strategy. You focus on modeling the new strategy and practice using the strategy together in a minilesson in which your instruction is transparent. Then you move the strategy work to independent and coached practice in the workshop. The minilesson is the key to explicit and purposeful instruction.

A minilesson is a carefully planned teaching moment in which you focus on one skill or strategy. As the year progresses you will naturally weave in previously taught strategies as well. Model your thinking for children and carefully show them how they will use the strategy for their own work. In the minilesson you want to wake up the children's brains and say, *Look here, you need to know this and I am going to show you how to think like this! Notice how I am thinking about, doing, or using this strategy. It is simple and useful, and you can do it too. When you do what I do, you will be a reader [or writer] too; you will be successful.*

FIGURE 6.1 Release-of-Responsibility Model

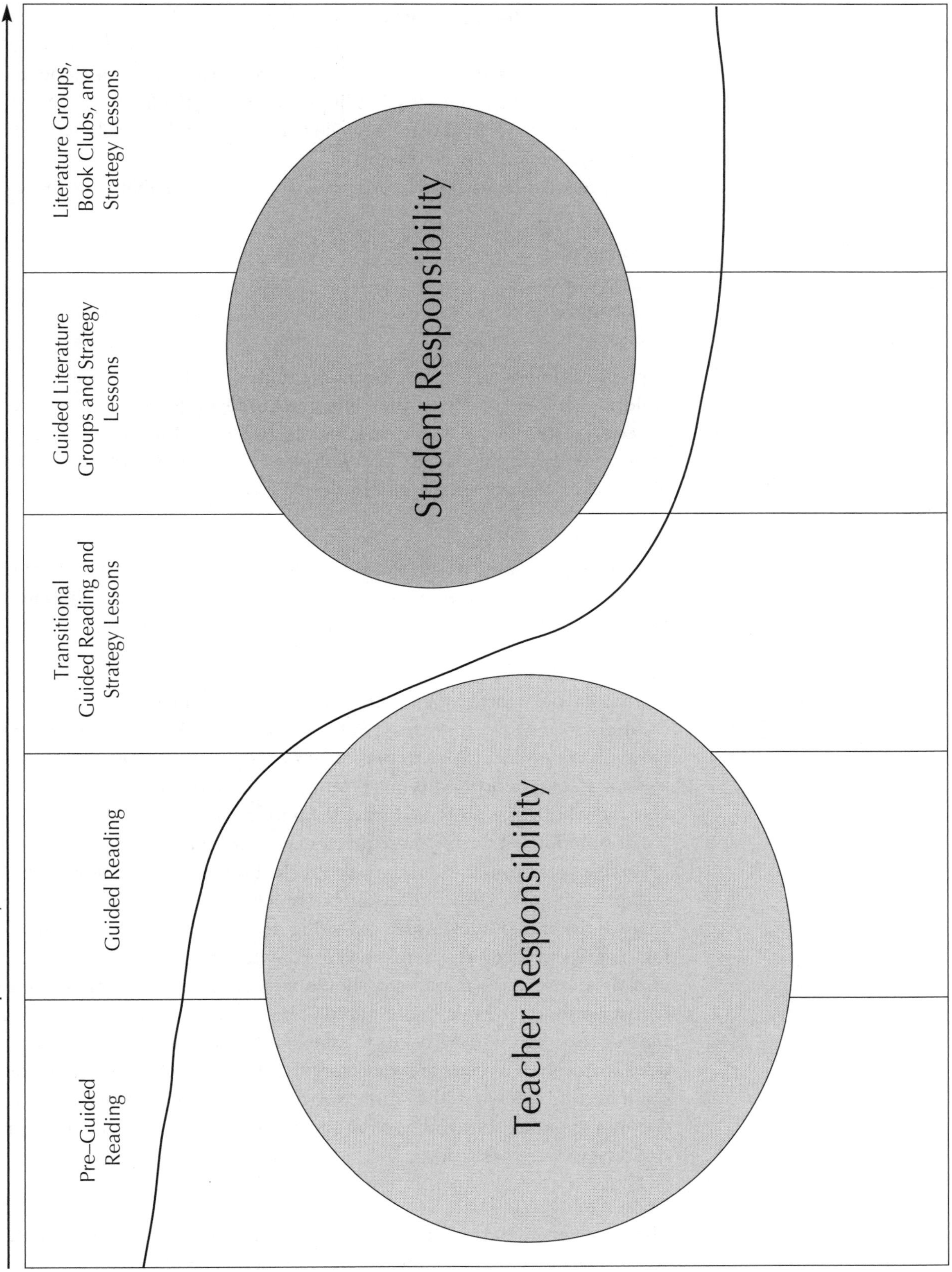

Pre–Guided
Reading

Guided Reading

Transitional
Guided Reading and
Strategy Lessons

Guided Literature
Groups and Strategy
Lessons

Literature Groups,
Book Clubs, and
Strategy Lessons

Student Responsibility

Teacher Responsibility

Workshops traditionally begin with minilessons, but your minilessons need to meet the needs of your students. Your minilessons should be concentrated tidbits of information that pack a powerful punch of student learning into just ten minutes. Yes, just ten minutes (well, maybe fifteen, but not much more than that). A well-structured minilesson shows children what to do, when, how, and why.

A precise minilesson has four parts (Figure 6.2 lays them out graphically for you):

- connection
- direct instruction
- engagement
- closure (Calkins 2001)

A precise minilesson teaches one point, models the same point, and shows children how they are to do the same thing independently. Be direct, be concise, create a visual to ensure students understand what you want them to do, and expect children to try the strategy during the workshop. Let's look at each component a bit more closely.

Connection
The initial part of the lesson prompts children to connect with their prior knowledge and tells them what they are going to do. It is very short and is therefore represented by a small box.

Direct instruction
During the next part of the minilesson, the body of the lesson, you show children one new idea, strategy, or skill, and you make your thinking transparent. You tell them, *This is what you need to know, this is what it looks like, and this is how you do it.* This box is larger, because this is how you will spend the bulk of your time during the minilesson.

It is important during these preciously short ten minutes not to elicit a lot of response from the children; you'll elicit some response during the engagement part of the minilesson, but much more during the whole-group share at the end of the workshop. During direct instruction, focus on teaching. There aren't enough minutes in the day to teach something the children already know, so the minilesson should introduce new learning or reinforce recent learning. The minilesson should present a skill, strategy, or idea that the majority of your class needs to know and understand, so there's no need to question or elicit answers from the children. If they know it, you don't need to teach it. If they don't know it, they can't be expected to know the answers until after you have taught a few lessons and given them practice time in the workshop.

Engagement
The engagement part of the minilesson may last only two or three minutes, so the engagement box on the lesson plan sheet is smaller than the direct

FIGURE 6.2 The Components of a Minilesson

Four-Block Minilesson Plan

1. Connection

2. Direct Instruction

3. Engagement

4. Closure

instruction one. During engagement you need to help children transfer information from their short-term memory to their long-term memory. What they learn in the minilesson may still be washed away after a few hours or days, but you don't want it to wash away the second you finish the lesson and the children move to their seats or special work areas. So, you *engage* them by having the children share with a partner (pair share). They may explain what they are going to do for the day, discuss a book, or remind each other of the steps in the writing process.

Closure

During the final step of the minilesson you provide closure. This is quick. You recap what the children said or did during engagement, point their minds back to the objective of the minilesson, and then send them off to the workshop to practice, to read, to write, and to learn.

Stay focused on what you are teaching

Effective minilessons teach *one* point, or objective, at a time. Effective minilessons scaffold student learning. In essence, minilessons focus on three steps:

- Tell the children what they need to know. (*Today we are going to learn to take notes on our nonfiction books about Native Americans because we are going to write reports on these books.*)
- Model what they need to know. (*Watch how I take a note on this page I read. I jot down a word or two—I don't write in complete sentences—then I put the sticky note on the page where I took the note.*)
- Tell them how you modeled what they need to know. (*I showed you how to take notes on your nonfiction books. When you take notes, you gather information that you will use later to write a report.*)

Notice how the minilesson in Figure 6.3 focuses the children on these three steps. The lesson guides the children by telling, showing, monitoring, and telling the same point over and over. By going deep, your minilessons scaffold children to learn the one point you are focused on.

Guided Reading Is a Teaching Moment

Guided reading is the ultimate teaching moment. During guided reading you are teaching children a fix-up or comprehension strategy paired with a leveled text. You may also focus on developing fluency. The intent of guided reading is to give children small-group direct instruction focused on helping them become independent readers (Optiz and Ford 2001). It is, of course, only one part of the literacy block, but it is the big moment when you are able to strategically match a reader to a text and *coach* him to read the text on his own.

FIGURE 6.3 Minilesson Plan Filled Out

Four-Block Minilesson Plan
Lesson: Text-to-Text Connections

1. Connection

"We have been making connections when we read books about things we remember. Today, I want to talk about connections we make to other texts, or books."

2. Direct Instruction

- Model a text-to-text connection with two mentor texts (choose class favorites).
- Write on a chart the definition of a t–t connection.
- Discuss your thinking while reading out loud. Show the children how one part in the book reminded you of another book.
- Discuss how the children can make t–t or text-to-self connections during the workshop. Encourage them to try t–t thinking.

3. Engagement

- Have the children turn knee-to-knee with a partner and share what a t–t connection is.
- Then have the children think of any books they can connect together—class favorites, mentor texts, or personal favorites.
- Have them turn knee-to-knee again and share their thinking about books.

4. Closure

Ask two children who discussed a connection between two books or texts to share their conversation aloud with the class. Remind the class what a t–t connection is and send them off to read.

During guided reading there is no round-robin reading and there is no correcting; instead, there is a considerable amount of showing, modeling, coaching, and guiding. Goals for guided reading instruction may include to

- acquire accuracy and fluency at a given text level
- acquire comprehension strategies
- read with prosody (rhythm and intonation)
- make meaning from a variety of texts and genres
- write about reading to develop comprehension
- use fix-up strategies accurately
- be motivated to read and be engaged as a reader
- provide a supportive context for children to practice strategies
- discuss meaning and understanding developed from text
- love to read

Planning your guided reading instruction

A lesson plan helps you organize information—which children are in the group, what level book they are reading, the focus of the lesson, how to teach the lesson, and notes on student progress. You can use a variety of forms to plan for guided reading. Figure 6.4 is a form that works well to plan guided reading for young children.

The form shown in Figure 6.5 can help you plan guided reading for children who are becoming fluent readers of chapter books or nonfiction texts with quite a bit of text on the page. This form includes a place to record vocabulary, comprehension questions, and a follow-up strategy.

Moving beyond guided reading

Often teachers ask, "When do I teach guided reading and when do I teach literature groups?" Well, that depends on the reading abilities and needs of your class. However, I believe it also depends on how much your students need to learn to close the achievement gap. The appropriate question may not be Should I teach guided reading *or* literature groups? There is a third choice that falls outside this either-or dichotomy.

Children who need support are often not ready for literature groups, not even in third grade. They still need a lot of guidance and encouragement to become readers. However, they are often ready to move beyond traditional guided reading. Consider what your children need and what they are ready to attempt, then modify your guided reading lessons accordingly.

Michael Optiz and Michael Ford consider multiple ways to stretch guided reading to meet students' needs in their book *Reaching Readers: Flexible and Innovative Strategies for Guided Reading* (2001). They discuss four types of guided reading grouping:

- whole class
- small group

FIGURE 6.4 Guided Reading Lesson Plan Form—Emergent Readers

Guided Reading Lesson Plan

Group: _____   Date: _____

Title of Book: _____   Level: _____

Focus (Strategy/Skill): _____

Word Work: _____

Name							Notes

Guided Reading Lesson

Group: _____

Lesson Focus: _____

Book Title: _____ Level: _____

Focus Strategy:

Vocabulary to Float:

Page:	Notes:
Page:	
Page:	
Page:	
Page:	
Page:	

Word Work:

Follow-Up:

FIGURE 6.5 Guided Reading Lesson Plan—Transitional Readers

- partners
- one-on-one

Which to use depends on your goals for student learning, the strategy you want to teach, and how much help children need. When you consider *all* your options, you can continue to offer children scaffolded instruction that grows as they grow.

Conferring Is a Teaching Moment

A guided reading conference is essentially a one-on-one reading group. While conferring, you can evaluate a student's understanding of how to use a strategy, monitor her ability to use fix-up strategies and comprehension strategies, note her progress on the leveled text gradient, and reteach when necessary.

Conferring is checking in. You can take anecdotal notes on individual student progress, take a running record, and give a child direction regarding his next step as a reader. You support a child during a guided reading conference. You help him focus by saying, *Let me hang out with you while you learn this . . . and then I can guide you when you get stuck.*

To teach well, you need to assess student needs frequently. During a conference you can note a child's ability to

- figure out unknown words
- use language conventions
- read fluently
- respond to text
- comprehend text
- use specific comprehension strategies

It is important to record the rich information you gather about children during a conference. You can gather notes in a binder or keep them in a file folder. One simple method is to keep a reading record notebook in each child's book box. Then when you meet with the child, the notebook is right there, and you don't have to carry the notebooks with you. In the notebook you record reading behavior, take a running record, note fluency and decoding abilities, note strategy use, note vocabulary development, and jot down any other observations. You can also give the child a goal and write the goal in the notebook. Figure 6.6 shows a reading record notebook. The goal is written on the sticker and placed where the child can refer back to it so that she can monitor her own reading progress.

Sideline Support

A few days ago I was cheering on my daughter as her team executed a beautiful defense move in a soccer game. For a moment I stopped concentrating on my daughter and the game and realized that all the soccer moms

FIGURE 6.6 Reading Record Notebook

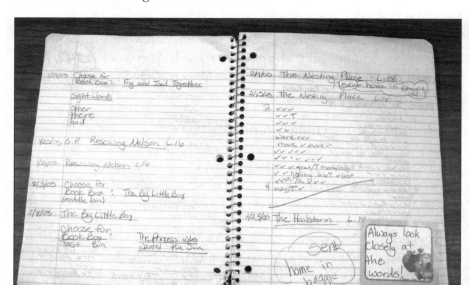

were on their feet, the dads poised just in front of us. We were all yelling encouragement, our voices ringing out over the field. "Go left!" "Give 'em a challenge!" "Way to go!" In the end, the other team scored. But even though our team lost the point, our encouraging words continued to echo across the field. "Great work." "Next time, cover the front." "Run back and get ready!" This immediate positive feedback conveyed to the girls that no matter how hard you try, sometimes the opponent scores. We were also encouraging the girls to redirect their energy and move on to the next strategy. The message: never stop trying and *Go! Go! Go!*

In the classroom we need to focus on *Go!* Too often our young children with limited literacy experience feel unsure about the text they are reading or the text they are creating. We need to be yelling with all our might *Go! Go! Go!* as they head into the end zone. Then we need to provide a quick response that encourages and redirects: "Next time you come to a word you don't know, look at the first sound and get your mouth ready. You can do it; you are such a smart reader."

We also need to remind ourselves to *Go! Go! Go!* and not be discouraged by the elements that we cannot control that affect our students' progress. We may not be able to do anything about what knowledge a child brings with her to school, but we certainly can make a world of difference once she settles in to read with her book box by her side.

Choose your stance and your words carefully. And encourage yourself to keep going.

CHAPTER SEVEN

When Your Students Can't Read Well

Predictable Problems, Possible Solutions

While trying to understand children's reading behavior can take a lifetime, the important thing is to collaborate with colleagues and share what you have learned along the way. Here are a few things I've learned. I know that it is overwhelming to organize guided reading groups, confer with every student, and ensure that children are reading just-right books all the time. I know that of the three things I just mentioned, guided reading groups are often the easiest to ignore. I know that sometimes it is easier to confer with children one-on-one about their reading strategies and determine whether they are reading a just-right book than it is to bring a group back to the table for a guided reading session. Why is that?

Well, during the many years I have coached teachers in guided reading techniques, I have noticed some fairly predictable problems:

- a few children may be making little progress and are not learning to read
- other children can read, but their use of strategies is erratic and they don't seem to retain the strategies they've been taught
- many children are reading just fine and their guided reading lessons seem mundane
- one or two children in the class are way ahead of everyone else, and challenging them is exhausting

I am going to address only the first two points, as they occur most frequently. When you are stretching to find ways to challenge students reading at or above grade level, you may consider moving them to higher reading levels while paying attention to the fluency and comprehension pointers presented in this chapter. When you are ready, you may want to read professional texts to deepen your practice and search for more answers. For a more in-depth look at reading processes overall, I suggest the following books:

■ *On Solid Ground: Strategies for Teaching Reading, K–3*, by Sharon Taberski (2000)
■ *Guided Reading: Good First Teaching for All Children*, by Irene C. Fountas and Gay Su Pinnell (1996)
■ *Change Over Time in Children's Literacy Development*, by Marie Clay (2001)

Coping with Pressure and Discouragement

The lowest point in the year is often midway through, right after winter break, when you are eager to see growth and tired because you have been at this for a while but the end is still a ways off. It is also the time of year when pressure related to accountability measures heats up. With that grand state test by which your school will be publicly judged looming on the horizon, it is little wonder you are feeling pressure; you want the children to perform well on an assessment like this.

Before we look at a few predictable issues related to children's reading progress, remember the goal of your instruction: you want children to learn to read. Obviously, it is important to give them direct instruction in decoding, fluency, and comprehension. And this instruction needs to occur in an environment that not only values wide reading but celebrates reading and expects reading to occur every day.

Avoid one-size-fits-all approaches and solutions. While I have identified a few general patterns that pop up in connection with children's reading progress, the possible solutions to help children continue growing lie in your professionalism and the individualized help you give kids every day. Yes, if you stay focused and provide children with the next steps they need when they need them, they will succeed and will read. Their growth will happen—and it will result in more than a good test score.

Target the Thinking Muscles

Let's look at children in different grades and the steps you can take to maintain a guided reading program without losing your mind. Remember that the best cure for the midyear doldrums is to look closely at what your students can do and then work on one new thing at a time. This way you won't overwhelm yourself or the children.

The possible solutions I offer incorporate six targets designed to make managing guided reading within your workshop easier. These targets are focused on moving children along the continuum of reading growth. Remember, you want the children's thinking muscles working—exercising the strategies, skills, and vocabulary and imprinting them in their memory.

Thinking-muscle targets include

■ putting children in the driver's seat—having them read and work with the text, *not* simply listen to you or another child read aloud

- having children sit with you as they read independently in a book just beyond what they can read alone
- previewing the book to orient children to the text and the possible pitfalls (or learning moments) they will encounter
- showing children a strategy to try with the book with the goal of turning that strategy into a skill
- encouraging children with positive statements about what they did right as readers
- avoiding discussing what children did wrong as readers and avoiding chastising them for a lack of focus or for forgetting

Some of My Students Aren't Learning to Read

It is February, and Lori has five students in her first-grade class who are reading at various below-grade levels, DRA level 2 to DRA level 5, and have improved very little since the beginning of the school year. The rest of the class is zooming on ahead, reading at about level 10, so Lori is anxious about helping the children in this group learn to read.

One child especially has Lori worried. Viviana is a vivacious girl with adorable curls and big brown eyes. During a parent conference, Viviana's mother confessed to having had trouble reading while growing up and being sent to a special class; she believed Viviana would also have trouble learning to read. Lori recognized these issues in the fall, but now that spring has come, she knows she needs to take vigorous action. Viviana came into first grade reading at DRA level 1 and is now reading at DRA level 2. End-of-year reading-level benchmarks as recommend by the Primary Literacy Standards include the following (New Standards Speaking and Listening Committee 2001):

- kindergarten: Fountas and Pinnell level C (DRA level 3)
- first grade: Fountas and Pinnell level I (DRA level 18)
- second grade: Fountas and Pinnell levels L–M (DRA level 24)
- third grade: Fountas and Pinnell levels O–P (DRA level 38)

Looking Closely at What Viviana Knows

Even though Viviana is struggling, she knows quite a bit about reading. In order to give Lori more direction, I work with Viviana so I can understand her as a reader, see what she can do as a reader. You can kick start student progress through formative assessment—carefully noting what a child can do as a reader and using this information to plan the next guided reading lesson.

In order to gather data on Viviana's reading ability, I give her a running record on a level B book that she has not previously read. I discover that Viviana knows that the words move from left to right, top to bottom. She tracks the words with her finger, although she doesn't do this consistently. Viviana also knows the difference between a word and a letter; she demonstrates this when I ask her to point to the last word in the first sentence and the first letter of the second word in that sentence.

I also notice that Viviana knows a few words on sight (*I*, *me*, and *is*) and understands the *I like* pattern in the book, a phrase she is able to read again and again after I preview it briefly. However, she doesn't know how to figure out words she doesn't know. She gets her mouth ready (forms the sound with her lips) but doesn't make the sound; instead, she hesitates and looks at me for help. Lori's assessments show that Viviana knows all of her letters and sounds, but she cannot apply this knowledge when reading a book. It is clear that Viviana needs focused help.

A Lesson That Guides and Supports

Viviana needs direct guidance in order to focus on decoding words in text and build her confidence as a reader. Together, Lori and Viviana will apply and practice what Viviana must learn. Lori brings Viviana back to the reading table with the two other students in this reading group. She has the book *I Can Jump*, by Joy Cowley (1986); a whiteboard; a cut-up sentence strip; and a marker. This lesson will focus on

- reading a book just beyond what Viviana can read on her own
- getting Viviana's thinking muscles working and promoting a productive learning cycle or flow (as Viviana works at the words, she will feel validated by her success and energized to keep going)
- tailoring the lesson so that it is just long enough to reinforce the learning cycle (instead of pushing Viviana too far so that she becomes discouraged or exhausted and shuts down)
- helping Viviana see patterns in words and learn to chunk words to apply the decoding strategy she knows
- extending Viviana's letter-sound knowledge so that she sees that the sounds work together in chunks, the decoding strategy supported by *I Can Jump* (the book does not lend itself to instruction in blending); it would do little good to teach Viviana a decoding strategy like chunking an onset and a rime without an immediate, purposeful way to practice, which she will do while reading the book during the lesson (not before or after)
- helping Viviana automatically recognize and use the three cueing systems

Teaching the Cueing Systems

Lori begins the lesson by showing Viviana's group the book *I Can Jump*. The lesson follows the general guidelines for a guided reading lesson:

- Discover what children might know about a book's contents by discussing the cover; if they know something about the book, activate their prior knowledge; if not, tell them what the book is about.
- Walk through the book; discuss the pictures as they relate to the text, point out specific words that will help children comprehend the text, and practice a decoding skill.
- Preview any other words children may not know.

- Remind children of the strategy or skill they will use when reading the book.
- Let children read the book on their own, working through the words themselves and not listening to other children read.
- Finish the reading by reinforcing good reading strategies children have attempted.
- End the lesson with word work that reinforces the decoding, vocabulary, or comprehension skill.

During the lesson Lori balances the children's need to share their ideas with her need to focus them on the text and practice a reading skill. This is important because often children who read far below grade level do *not* focus, and any discussion they instigate takes the lesson woefully off track. Although there are two other children in Viviana's group, my purpose here is to demonstrate what Lori does to help Viviana grasp a reading strategy.

Viviana looks intently at the cover of the book for about thirty seconds while Lori discusses the story they are going to read today. Then in her vibrant way, Viviana raises her hand, wiggling it emphatically while chanting, "Teacher, teacher . . . ."

Lori calmly places her hand over Viviana's other hand and says, "Just a minute, Viviana; first I need you to listen to me and think about what we are going to do together. OK?"

Viviana nods her head and looks back at her book. Lori begins to discuss the cover of the book, which has an illustration of a grasshopper. She asks the children to take their two pointer fingers and frame the word *jump*. Then she has the children turn to the title page, which has the same picture of a grasshopper. She asks them several questions about the picture, bringing out ideas that will help them understand the text. When the children's comments stray from the main idea, Lori gently brings their conversation back to the book. Lori wants the children to remember the text, so that as they read independently, they can use this discussion to help them read.

Now Lori asks the children to frame the word *grasshopper* on the first page of text. Viviana finds the small word *grass* in this big word, and another child finds the small word *hop*, a strategy they have been practicing together. Perfect! Lori wants to jump from this strategy to chunking words based on their onset and rime. Lori continues previewing the first few pages of the text, and the children practice finding small words in the big words. During the preview, Lori continually repeats the pattern in the book: "Oh, so the bug might say, 'I can jump.' I notice the word *said* is on the page . . . so I bet we are right!"

Then Lori asks the children to read independently while they remain at the table. Lori moves about the table, listening to each child and noting how well she or he is able to handle the text.

Viviana sails through the title page, but she gets stuck on the word *said* on the first page. The text reads, "'I can jump,' said the grasshopper."

Viviana looks at the word, focuses on the first letter, and says /s/. She stops and waits for a long time. Lori intervenes and says, "If you can't sound it out, skip it and come back to it." Viviana reads to the end of the two-page spread. Then Lori points to the word *said*: "What do you think the word could be? Maybe you already know the word. Let's read the sentence and skip the word and then think if we know a word that begins with /s/ that will make sense right here."

Viviana reads, "'I can jump,' /s/ the grasshopper."

"What do you think the word would be, Viviana?"

Viviana tries the sentence again, and she gets it. "*Said*. That is *said*."

"Right! Now keep going."

On the next page Viviana reads, "'I can run,' said the spider. 'I can hop,' /s/ [*she stops, then keeps going*] the frog." She then goes back and reads the word correctly as *said*.

Lori reinforces Viviana's strategy. "Oh, you went back and fixed it up. Great!"

When the children are done reading, Lori has them focus on learning a new skill, chunking words based on the onset and the rime. She shows the rime -*ump* on the whiteboard. Then she writes down the words *lump*, *dump*, *jump*, *hump*, and *pump*, passes out magnetic letters, and has the children form the words. She follows this sequence:

■ Make the rime -*ump*.
■ Place one letter in front of the chunk, or rime.
■ Say the word formed. For example, add a *p*, then say *pump*.
■ Say the sound of each letter.
■ Say the word.
■ Say the rime -*ump*.
■ Mix up the letters and rebuild the word.
■ Then give a new letter for the onset—*j*, for example.
■ Finish by writing a few words on small vocabulary cards and placing the cards in the children's book box for practice: *jump*, *lump*, *pump*, *hump*.

Lori reinforces the word work with these statements:

■ Don't say the letters; say the sounds.
■ Look for the chunk (the rime).
■ Get your mouth ready for the first sound.
■ Check the last letter of the word. What is the sound it makes? (Some children forget the chunk. Viviana keeps saying *hunt*.)
■ Try it again and point to the word when you say it.
■ You fixed it yourself!

Further resources for word work at any level include

■ *Words Their Way: Word Study for Phonics, Vocabulary, and Spelling Instruction*, 3d ed., by Donald R. Bear, Marcia Invernizzi, Shane R. Templeton, and Francine Johnston (1996)

- *Word Matters*, by Irene C. Fountas and Gay Su Pinnell (1998)
- *Phonics Lessons: Letters, Words, and How They Work, Grade 1*, by Gay Su Pinnell and Irene C. Fountas (2003)
- *Phonics Lessons: Letters, Words, and How They Work, Grade 2*, by Gay Su Pinnell and Irene C. Fountas (2003)
- *Word Study Lessons: Phonics, Spelling, and Vocabulary*, by Irene C. Fountas and Gay Su Pinnell (2004)

My Students Can Read, but Their Use of Strategies Is Erratic

In February my second-grade teachers (including Hollie and Pam, whose classrooms are highlighted in Chapters 2 and 4) met with me to evaluate where their children were as a group of readers. Our goal was to pinpoint which children were doing well and which children needed a bit of extra support. The second-grade team listed a few issues their students were grappling with as readers:

- Children reading at or above grade level needed to work on comprehension strategies.
- A group of children reading at grade level were just calling words, not *comprehending*; they were not truly reading and interacting with text.
- A few children were rushing through text and not consistently applying fix-up strategies.
- Some children were not reading fluently; their reading was laborious even though they read all the words correctly. A few others were reading so quickly that they misread many words, skipped words, and read like robots.
- Many English learners were using reading strategies effectively but not at the level of fluency expected at this point in the school year. They read orally word by word, and their comprehension was weak.
- Some children, both English learners and non–English learners, didn't have the vocabulary to understand what they were reading. They might decode accurately and fluently and understand the gist of the text, but they missed important ideas that hinged on one or two key words.

Possible Solutions for Struggling Readers

The first step is to commit to action. If your guided reading groups are not meeting frequently enough, make it happen. If you have not conferred one-on-one with your struggling readers two or three times during the month, make it happen. If the children are not spending approximately thirty minutes in sustained reading, make it happen. If the group lessons in word study and spelling have not been precise and focused on students knowing, doing, and interacting with words, change your instructional stance. In other words, before scrambling to add something *new* to your routine, ensure that the routine you have in place is humming along.

Once all of these things are in place, you need to be sure that children understand what they read. Make connections between the information in the book they are reading and their vocabulary to ensure that children are learning words and the concepts those words represent. Focus on

- a working knowledge of phonemes and how words work
- sustained reading
- fluency during oral reading, including reading rate and the ability to read with prosody (rhythm and intonation)
- comprehension strategies
- vocabulary development

Phonemic knowledge

Children's awareness of the phonemic structure of words is a strong predictor of their success in learning to read (Adams 1990). But a more important predictor is their understanding of how words work *together*. Children's conscious knowledge of phonemes is important. While children apply phonemic knowledge to figure out unknown words, they also use this knowledge to discriminate between words (for example, words that are spelled and pronounced alike but have slightly different meanings: "I'll *lead* the class to the cafeteria" and "He is the *lead* singer in the band").

A deep and thorough knowledge of the letters and spelling patterns that make up words is extremely important for skillful and successful reading. This is the goal of good phonics instruction, which provides direct opportunities to learn letters and sounds and how these letters and sounds are grouped into words. In addition, good phonics instruction provides this information in contexts in which children can *apply* this knowledge and build a conscious understanding of letter sounds and words. Synthetic phonics—phonics that is unconnected to context—should be used very sparingly (NICHD 2000).

Keep your eye on the ball. The goal of phonics instruction is to help children read well and enjoy reading, so teach enough phonemic awareness and phonics skills to help children begin reading in *real books*. Don't get swamped by workbook pages on phonics. Research shows that this kind of exercise isn't effective (Adams 1990; NICHD 2000). Teach key knowledge and skills and ensure students can apply that knowledge in reading and writing by focusing on analogy phonics or analytic phonics (see Figure 7.1).

Programs that focus too much on the teaching of letter-sound relationships and not enough on putting *this knowledge to work* are ineffective. Help your students understand the purpose of learning letter sounds, which is to use this knowledge in their daily reading and writing.

Sustained reading

Children don't spend enough time reading in class, and readers who need support spend even *less* time reading at school (Allington 2001; Adams 1990). These children *need* to be reading. Don't give them less time because they are struggling. Less practice is the *opposite* of what they need. The more disabled readers are, the more time they need to spend reading. Struggling readers need additional bottom time—time spent in a chair, book in hand, reading. All children need this time, and while less able readers may need extra time to learn to focus, this does not mean they can't handle the workshop format.

Worksheet activities need to take a backseat during the workshop, as they rarely meet the individual needs of the child and take up precious time that should be spent reading. Many studies show that struggling readers spend less time reading and more time filling out worksheets, particularly worksheets that reinforce phonics skills (Adams 1990; McGill-Franzen, Zmack, Solic, and Zeig 2006). These children need the opportunity to apply and practice the letter-sound skills taught to them during guided reading. As they learn more words, they will be able to use patterns and analogies to figure out unknown words (Cunningham and Cunningham 2002).

Studies show that the amount of reading a child does directly impacts how that child processes words. Samuels, LaBerge, and Bremer (1978) discovered that less able second-grade readers who had the least experience with reading used letter-by-letter processing to figure out unknown words. More able fourth-grade readers focused on word parts of more than one letter. More experienced sixth-grade readers began to focus on words in their entirety. There appears to be a strong correlation between readers' ability to decode unknown words and the size of the unit (a single letter, a cluster of letters, or the whole word) they attend to.

FIGURE 7.1 Types of Phonics Instruction

Phonics instruction stresses letter-sound correspondences and their use in reading and spelling. There are several types of phonics instruction:

- *Analogy phonics*: teaching unfamiliar words by analogy to known words
- *Analytic phonics*: teaching how to analyze letter-sound relationships in previously learned words to avoid pronouncing sounds in isolation in new words
- *Embedded phonics*: teaching phonics skills in connection with reading books, a more implicit approach that relies somewhat on incidental learning
- *Phonics through spelling*: teaching how to segment words into phonemes and to select letters for those phonemes (teaching phonetic spelling)
- *Synthetic phonics*: explicitly teaching how to convert letters into sounds and then blend the sounds into words

Fluency

Low-achieving or struggling readers spend more time reading aloud than able readers do, and this can easily become the only focus. Struggling readers need encouragement and opportunities to examine the structure of texts and think about the *meaning* of texts. When working with these readers, choose a few words on which to focus and then move quickly to examining what the text means.

The more children read in a just-right book, the more they will be able to interact with strategies. Just-right books enable readers to read *more* books with greater success; this exposes them to a larger number of words. To develop a vocabulary of words they recognize on sight, they need to be exposed to large numbers of words and see how words relate to one another. This happens naturally during sustained reading (Nagy and Anderson 1984; Stahl 1999).

Fluency instruction for struggling readers should focus on the development of speed, accuracy, and proper expression (NICHD 2000). Fluency is important because it directly affects comprehension (Samuels 2002). When children can identify words quickly and easily, their mind is free to focus on understanding the text.

Repeated reading (not just *oral* repeated reading) helps children develop fluency. Children move through three general stages of word recognition (Samuels 2002):

- *Nonaccurate*: They have difficulty identifying words in an unknown text.
- *Accurate but not automatic*: They can read some words on sight and figure out others by sounding them out, but their oral reading is delivered in a monotone and they have little recall of what they've read.
- *Accurate and automatic (fluent)*: They read orally with speed, accuracy, and normal expression; they sound as if they are talking.

Children need the opportunity to read a text many times before reading it aloud if they are going to be judged on fluency. This is the perfect reason to slip texts from previous guided reading lessons into their book boxes. You can also have children listen to a book being read aloud more than once. A simple and smart way to use technology is to record selected texts using your classroom computers' multimedia software and let children listen to the recording through headphones while they read along with the text. Reading along with the recording like this, children are able to practice with a "coach": they hear the pronunciation of unknown words, listen to voice inflection, and imprint the reading pace on their consciousness. Essentially, they are reading with the coach what they cannot read alone—practicing fluency.

When you want to check whether a student is fluent at a particular level, have him read aloud to you. Notice the miscues he makes. When he is finished, ask him to briefly retell the passage. Fluent readers will understand what they read as well as read accurately and with expression.

Fluency is developed in three ways:

- repeated opportunities to read *at an independent level*
- repeated opportunities for specific instruction in decoding skills (e.g., chunking)
- repeated paired readings, when two students read short texts out loud together

Comprehension strategies

Good readers and writers create meaning. They select and use appropriate reading strategies, monitor their understanding while they read, and refine their understanding as they think about (and write about) what they have read. Our job is to help them become aware of each strategy they are using, talk with them about how well they are doing with a particular strategy, and then give them ample time to read so that the strategy becomes part of their unconscious reading process. In order to avoid predictable problems in the workshop, ensure that your minilessons are focused on the strategies you are teaching. Don't throw too much into one lesson, and don't bounce around from strategy to strategy. Give your students time to learn each strategy well before insisting they move on to another. (See Chapter 6 for a description of research-based reading strategies to introduce into the workshop.)

Vocabulary development

There are three important issues related to vocabulary development:

- There is a vocabulary gap between students in different socioeconomic groups.
- Vocabulary knowledge affects long-term student achievement.
- Vocabulary growth cumulates over time.

Our vocabularies comprise more than just the number of words we know. Think of vocabulary knowledge like this:

- the number of words we know (size)
- familiarity with the topics connected to the words (breadth)
- familiarity with ideas related to the topics (depth)

These aspects of our vocabulary directly affect our ability to read well, discuss ideas, write well, and understand academic conversations.

We need to pay attention to our students' word learning. A large vocabulary is positively correlated with reading comprehension and reading ability after third grade. The more words children know, the more children can comprehend what they read and therefore increase their knowledge. Knowing words creates opportunities *to learn more words.*

Principles of vocabulary instruction include

- creating a word-rich learning environment
- making connections to and between words

- engaging students with explicit instruction
- accelerating vocabulary development through wide reading

Now What? These Third-Grade Readers Need More Support

When our school's third-grade team met to discuss the reading issues their students were dealing with, they mentioned many of the ones the second-grade team had but added several more:

- reading approximately two years behind grade level
- learning English and the ways of a new country
- learning to chunk by identifying root words, prefixes, and suffixes
- blending initial, medial, and final sounds together when decoding unknown words
- applying a repertoire of reading strategies to longer texts and content textbooks
- comprehending what they were reading
- using story elements as an organizing structure for comprehension
- using nonfiction conventions of print as a structure to understand the material
- identifying theme

Possible Solutions for Struggling Readers in Third Grade

The first step to take when brainstorming possible solutions for struggling third-grade students is to take a long hard look at your assessments, then take a long hard look at your instruction, and answer this question: Does your instruction match student needs?

It is important to match student needs with the right fix-up strategies and comprehension strategies. As children deepen their conceptual understanding of how words and language are constructed, they need to increase their ability to figure out unknown words, independently add words to their vocabulary, and regulate their reading through self-sustaining skills that help them maintain fluency and concentrate on meaning (Clay 2001; Stahl 1999).

Fix-up strategies

Fix-up strategies for third graders include

- looking for root words and thinking about other words that are similar to the root word
- understanding how affixes change the meanings of root words, and then applying this knowledge to unknown words
- thinking of word families in order to deduce the meaning or the pronunciation of a new word
- thinking about words with multiple meanings and matching a meaning to the text

- thinking about sentence structure (syntax) and whether or not what they read looks right and sounds right
- thinking of homonyms, antonyms, and synonyms when trying to determine the meaning of unknown words
- using a dictionary and/or thesaurus to look up words that they *almost* know but are not sure of the exact meaning of
- reading abundantly and frequently

Comprehension strategies

Third graders are developing their repertoire of comprehension strategies. Children who are at risk and need additional support may not yet be fluent or proficient readers in grade-level material. While instinctively it may seem that focusing on fix-up strategies (including phonics) is what they need, this is not necessarily true. At-risk readers in third grade need to connect to the *meaning* of texts and need to develop independent strategies to make meaning when they read. It is imperative that nine-year-olds have a few self-sustaining comprehension strategies in place or they will not develop as readers. While a proficient reader interweaves all the following strategies when reading a grade-level text, an at-risk reader may apply a strategy only sporadically or may not have a conscious understanding of how good readers use the strategy.

Comprehension strategies to focus on include (South Carolina State Department of Education 2007; California State Department of Education 2007):

- making connections (text to self, text to text, text to world)
- summarizing, focusing specifically on details and theme
- asking and answering questions while reading
- making predictions about character actions, plot, and problem solving
- drawing conclusions and making inferences
- categorizing and classifying information in nonfiction texts
- identifying cause and effect in relation to character actions, thoughts, and plot
- differentiating between fact and opinion in nonfiction texts
- using graphic organizers to understand text and organize information in texts
- comparing and contrasting characters, setting, events, and ideas within and among a variety of texts
- comparing and contrasting information and elements within a single text
- identifying problem → solution in fiction
- distinguishing between fiction and nonfiction
- identifying the author's purpose for writing a particular piece

Self-assessment strategies

Children who need support in third grade should work to develop self-assessment strategies. Soon they will be in larger classes with a higher concentration of content studies. And soon after that they will be in middle school, where they may be changing classes and teachers each period. Self-assessment strategies, like other strategies in students' invisible backpacks, can help students survive and thrive long after they leave your classroom.

A simple yet effective self-assessment strategy is a reading checklist. Afflerbach (2002) recommends a reading checklist that children can use in third grade and beyond (see Figure 7.2). A self-assessment checklist like this helps children understand their own use of a strategy and focus on building and owning a repertoire of strategies. Essentially, the self-assessment checklist helps children determine whether a strategy is in their backpack (see Chapter 6).

Teach children how to use the reading checklist in a series of mini-lessons. Carefully think out loud as you show children how you use the checklist. Displaying the checklist on a big chart will remind children to use it and *how* to use it (Afflerbach 2002). Encourage students to make the checklist part of their daily reading life.

Another way to build third graders' independence and improve their reading skills is to focus on performance assessment. For a performance assessment, a child has to *do* something; your assessment of her skill is gleaned during her performance. Performance assessment offers the opportunity for you to see your students in action. Multiple-choice assessments tell you what a student can do on a specific reading passage at a specific time, but a performance assessment reveals how students are developing the complex thinking and processing required of the more sophisticated reading tasks they face as they grow (Afflerbach 2002).

Performance assessments are opportunities for third graders to think about their thinking and learning, to develop metacognitive strategies that help them improve as readers. For example, if you have taught a unit on making text connections, ask students to think about and describe their understanding of text connections and how often they make connections while reading. After teaching a unit on visualization, ask students to record how often they are visualizing while reading and write about what they see in their minds. Performance assessment results can help you guide children to create their own reading goals. For example, *Last week I didn't do a good job thinking of my connections and jotting them down. This week when I read this new book, I am going to write at least five connections in my notebook.*

An easy-to-use performance assessment is a rubric students can use to rate themselves on their reading, thinking, responding, and understanding during a specific reading task (Afflerbach 2002). The children score themselves on how well they know, understand, and can apply a specific comprehension strategy. You can create a rubric like the one in Figure 7.3 for any unit of study.

FIGURE 7.2 Self-Assessment Checklist for Making Connections

My Reading Goal—Text Connections

After you finish each paragraph, focus on your goal: Making Text Connections.

_____ I remember why I am reading.

_____ I stop at the end of each paragraph to think about text connections—can I make any?

_____ I ask myself, "Does that connection make sense?" and "How do I know it makes sense?"

_____ I ask myself, "Is this a deep connection or a surface connection?"

_____ I remind myself to jot one or two connections in my notebook.

FIGURE 7.3 Rubric for Text Connections

My Reading Rubric—Text Connections

After you finish reading and responding, rate yourself:

⚡ ☺ 🚫	I made several text connections while reading.
⚡ ☺ 🚫	I wrote the connections down in my notebook.
⚡ ☺ 🚫	I focused on deep connections including: cause and effect (nonfiction) character thoughts and actions (fiction)
⚡ ☺ 🚫	I understand what a connection is; I can explain it with examples to my book partner.

Key

⚡ I am zooming! I do this well.

☺ I am doing OK, but still learning this.

🚫 Nope, I don't do this yet.

CHAPTER EIGHT

Helping English Learners in the Reading Workshop

Children who are learning English have the same capacity to learn grade-level material as all the other children in your classroom. If they participate in powerful and appropriate school experiences, receive focused intervention, and know that their teachers have high expectations, they can achieve at the same levels as children who are proficient in English or speak English as their first language. It just takes a classroom that supports language learning. My book *Help! My Kids Don't All Speak English* (2006) highlights classroom procedures and routines that support children and help them acquire English during the reading workshop.

Following are the key features of language classrooms:

- Language is taught through content.
- Collaborative learning is central to the minilessons.
- Students are allowed to speak or write in their primary language to communicate their understanding of the concepts taught in the minilessons.
- Reading, writing, listening, and speaking are developed in each lesson.
- Children are allowed to grow, to improve their English language skills by using English in appropriate and interactive ways.

Characteristics of English Learners

You may have children in your classroom who are just beginning to learn English or who can speak English but don't seem to be able to have meaningful conversations or understand the lessons. In both cases, I often hear teachers say, "Oh, it's a language problem." But what does that mean? You may want to consider the following:

- Does the child interact during the lessons and activities but not perform well on paper-and-pencil tests?

- What does a running record reveal about the child's ability to read in English?
- Does the child participate when it's time to share?
- Is the child using language to communicate and learn?

It is also important to consider how you have set up your reading workshop and the scaffolds you have in place to support children who are learning English. You have to deliberately create opportunities for these young learners to hear, see, and write English in a comfortable, nonthreatening environment.

Some children may be reading and writing in English but talking with classmates (and perhaps thinking) in their first language. This is perfectly normal and should be encouraged as long as it helps the children read, write, and respond to texts. After rehearsing their thoughts and ideas in their first language, they can later share these thoughts and ideas in English. The first language is a scaffold for comprehension, acquisition, and engagement.

The Functions of Language

During direct instruction, we may think we are being clear and simple enough for our English learners while in reality we are using language in ways in which these children may not be proficient. Functions of language we use during minilessons include the following (Gibbons 1991, 2002).

- classifying
- explaining
- comparing
- giving directions or commanding
- describing
- identifying
- planning and predicting
- sequencing
- questioning
- evaluating
- expressing position
- explaining
- hypothesizing
- inferring
- reporting
- suggesting

When children engage with information and share their thinking with a partner or the whole class, they are using these functions of language:

- agreeing and disagreeing
- comprehending
- classifying
- describing
- evaluating
- expressing likes and dislikes
- expressing identity
- hypothesizing
- summarizing
- inferring
- planning
- predicting
- reporting
- suggesting
- wishing and hoping

After the minilesson, as children read, write, talk, and listen, alone and with peers, they are using the following language functions:

- describing
- summarizing

- hypothesizing
- analyzing
- expressing opinion

If children have not yet acquired the language to perform these functions, we must scaffold the functions by helping them to acquire the language they need to participate in the lesson.

Helping English Learners Develop Language Functions

As we have seen, children use language for a variety of functions: to understand the curriculum (the propositional function), to interact with their peers and the teacher (the social function), and to communicate their thoughts, feelings, and attitudes (the expressive function). They also need to become familiar with the way their teachers use language and what teachers expect them to do during a specific activity. As English learners become more proficient in their new language and begin to understand what is expected of them as learners, they will become more fluent socially as well as academically. But keep in mind that even when they understand the academic demands of a lesson, they may not be able to speak English properly or effectively for quite some time. The more opportunities they have to speak English and the more comfortable they are about accepting the support of their teacher and their peers when they try to do so, the faster their English-speaking ability will develop.

English learners develop all three language functions at the same time: the functions are concurrent. While they may be able to control English socially before they develop academic proficiency in it, they nevertheless acquire academic English *as* they are mastering social English on the playground, as long as they are taught with methods that encourage language acquisition. It takes longer to understand and acquire what we think of as the functions and vocabulary of school language. And it takes five, six, seven, or more years to become fluent English speakers in all dimensions, social and academic.

Developing Academic Vocabulary

As children learn English, they acquire specific academic vocabulary (words belonging to a specific content area, like *mountainous* and *chlorophyll*) and general academic vocabulary (words not often used during everyday conversation but seen and heard in general classroom life, like *classify*, *summary*, and *organization*).

Children who are not English learners must also learn vocabulary and curriculum, but doing so in a second language is different (and more difficult) than it is in one's first language, because some of the semantic and syntactic information of the language does not come naturally, as it does in a first language. English learners have to build their academic vocabulary and knowledge base while acquiring English (AERA 2004b; Cummins 1989, 1991, 2003; Scarcella 2003).

English learners are developing the conversational skills and language they need to get along socially while also trying to navigate a sea of classroom words that might not make much sense. Often the language is so incomprehensible (and even when the words themselves are familiar, they may not make sense) that they are not ready to participate in reading workshop or partner shares; they simply tune out, refusing (being unable, really) to talk or write. Immersing children in language does not mean they will automatically pick up academic vocabulary. English learners need specific support that helps them understand what is going on in the classroom.

Language classrooms are not quiet classrooms. Children acquire personal and academic language *as they use language for real purposes*. Real purposes occur daily in the reading workshop as children think about and become familiar with reading comprehension strategies, apply these strategies to texts, and share their thoughts or questions about a text. This is an appropriate and encouraging environment in which to learn English as a second language.

Language Is a Window into Meaning

Often we teach as if language is a transparent medium for conveying what we want children to do. During a minilesson we talk to and with children and ask them to discuss their thinking with a partner; then we send them off to read and write independently, assuming that if they have been listening, they will know what to do. And children who speak English well complete their work easily: they understand what has been said; the expectations and language are transparent. But for English learners, the language is not transparent and the workshop can be challenging.

Language is the medium through which we communicate knowledge (Henze and Arriaza 2006). As teachers we share information, instruct, confer, and describe. We must be sure the language we use is transparent, not opaque. What we say must be clear and comprehensible to our students.

The first step toward helping English language learners in the reading workshop is to make sure our instruction is comprehensible. In other words, we need to have a specific purpose for teaching a particular lesson, explain the concept or strategy clearly, and make sure *all* students understand what we say, read, or write as we do so (Gibbons 1991, 2002). As we share information and hold conferences, we need to speak more slowly, pause more often, provide more visuals, offer more than one example, and break tasks into smaller steps (Richgels 2004).

Reading Workshop Outcomes

Children unfamiliar with academic (and perhaps social) English won't necessarily get the language and conventions of reading workshop just by being immersed in them. We have to explain them, model them, make them apparent. A workshop needs to have clear outcomes for English learners. While the routines are progressive, the context needs to model language structures and conventions, perhaps in a more traditional format. We need to explicitly model and reinforce what good readers read and how they act, think, sit, and connect while reading. The overall goal is for English learners to learn language and how to use it appropriately in order to participate fully in school and in the world.

Minilesson Outcomes

As described in Chapter 3, the workshop minilesson has four parts. Most of the language work occurs during the direct instruction and engagement portions of the lesson. During the direct instruction portion, teachers need to

- model thinking about reading
- model linguistic features common to talking about reading
- model linguistic features common to narratives and nonfiction texts
- model reading strategies

    During the engagement portion, children must be able to

- speak with peers about texts, strategies, vocabulary, and thinking
- follow and participate in the guided teacher conversation
- use specific vocabulary

Book Box Outcomes

Book boxes (also discussed in Chapter 3) support students' reading ability, their immersion in literary life, and their acquisition of language and content. When children are working with book boxes, you want them to know and understand how to

- browse and read for a sustained period of time
- self-select texts that are just right
- choose content-rich books that capture their interest
- read at length in several independent-level and instructional-level texts
- persevere through a text independently after a guided reading lesson
- become aware of cultural activities portrayed in texts (birthdays, trips to the park, trips to the zoo, soccer games)

Overall Reading Outcomes

Your English learners need to focus on

- breaking the print-sound code
- realizing that text carries meaning
- detecting the structural differences between genres
- understanding how words work, including spelling patterns, onset and rime patterns, and morphological patterns
- questioning the text ("I wonder why . . .")

- making and confirming predictions about the text
- skimming the text to prepare for reading
- using linking strategies to understand unfamiliar words ("If I know a word and it looks similar to another word I don't know, I can compare the two words and figure out the new word.")
- reading for detail and meaning
- summarizing and retelling

Reading Response Journal Outcomes

When children write about their reading, they are connecting with and thinking about texts. This can be difficult for children not fluent in English, and they will need support. This kind of authentic writing and response fosters language acquisition. During reading response, English learners focus on

- getting their ideas on paper
- drawing pictures if necessary
- matching sounds to words
- writing quickly without worrying about conventions (otherwise they will get stuck on making the sentences sound right and become paralyzed as writers)
- writing a lot (the more they write, the better they will become at sharing a connection, stating their opinion about a book, or sharing information)

Children at intermediate stages of learning English can go back and fix up their writing after initially getting their ideas down. Since they have acquired some English language skills, they may also be ready to venture into discussion, analysis, and reporting. However, these are higher-order skills, and English learners often don't yet control the expected verb tenses. Frames may help them kick start their thinking and writing. They will also benefit from charts that model the use of the past tense, the progressive past tense, and the progressive tense. Charts like these should be authentic; that is, they should be used in connection with an actual reading response (perhaps written by the teacher), not merely present rote verb conjugations. Remember to focus on language modeling and acquisition, not language learning.

English learners with intermediate skills should focus on

- using connective words (*then, later, next, afterward*)
- developing a written discussion they can share with a partner or the class
- using response frames (see the appendix) to guide writing and thinking

Supporting Vocabulary Growth in Reading Workshop

English learners benefit from vocabulary practice tailored to their specific needs. Two quick ways to provide this support are word rings and sight-word lists.

Word Rings

A word ring is made from small index cards and a metal ring. Punch a hole in the upper left-hand corner of a bunch of index cards and slip the cards on a metal ring (sold at office supply stores). Write, or have the children write, a vocabulary word on one side of each card; on the other side glue or draw a picture illustrating the word, write a synonym for the word, or give a short description of the word. Include verbs, general nouns, and content-specific vocabulary the children have trouble with in their reading and in their response journals. Specific choices will depend on how much English a child knows. Children new to English will need basic vocabulary on their word rings. The key is for a child to have a word ring of personalized words that she reviews from time to time.

Sight-Word Lists

Practicing recognizing words on sight is an excellent way to help children learn a new language. Write words taken from the books they are reading (independently or in guided reading) or from some other source on the word-list sheet in the appendix. (See page 177; you can copy this sheet on tagboard and have students store the lists in their book boxes.) Focus on eight, nine, or ten words at a time. As children add these words to their vocabularies, create a new list.

Adjusting Reading Workshop Instruction to English Learners' Ability

The English language learners in your classroom will naturally vary in ability. Some may be at the beginning stages of learning English, and others may seem fluent. Giving them many opportunities to listen to and participate in casual and academic conversations will help them acquire both social and school language. Remember, too, that English learners may not know enough about the culture or interpersonal situations being depicted in leveled texts to use the pictures and words to predict the story. In any case, you need to adjust your instruction to match your students' abilities.

Case Study: Emergent Reader

Karina is at the beginning stage of English language acquisition. She is quiet during the minilesson and usually chooses a spot near the back of the group. She often plays with the straps on her shoes or the tufts on the carpet and avoids eye contact with her teacher and with her peers. When it is time to share with a partner, the teacher has to prompt her repeatedly to do so. When it is time for independent reading, Karina hurries to a remote corner of the room. She looks through her books silently and quickly, turning the pages rapidly and hardly pausing to notice the pictures. When the teacher calls her to a guided reading lesson, Katrina walks slowly to the table and doesn't say very much during the lesson.

Suggestions for Karina's Instruction

- Read poetry and sing songs.
- Use a response frame (see the examples in the appendix) to help her focus on producing text in an emotionally safe but fun way.
- Provide a great many shared reading experiences that focus on
    - graphophonic symbols
    - sound-symbol relationships
    - picture cards or books with large pictures that support the text
    - key words that carry the most information in leveled text (see Fountas and Pinnell's levels A–C)
    - the link between thinking and pictures, cultural knowledge, and language knowledge
    - innovations on picture books, such as covering the words and having her use the pictures to write her own story
- Create a word ring featuring words she finds particularly useful or interesting.

Case Study: Intermediate Fluency

José entered kindergarten as an English learner; he is now in third grade and functions well in the classroom. His favorite subject is math. He says that reading and writing are OK but just a bit hard. During guided reading José raises his hand, indicating he wants to participate in the discussion, but he often doesn't say anything when it is his turn and allows another student to speak instead. When he does speak during group share, he talks around ideas (a common issue for English learners with limited vocabularies) and has trouble using exact words to retell a story. He hesitates often and waits for the teacher or another student to supply a word he cannot remember or doesn't know. When he writes about reading, he makes convention errors and his sentences meander. He is able to participate in writing reflections, but his thinking is imprecise.

Suggestions for José's Instruction

Provide a great many literacy experiences that focus on

- contextualized language using pictures, maps, videos, audiotapes, realia, and manipulatives
- opportunities to speak in small groups or with a partner
- shared reading of books and poetry
- intensive vocabulary development (Strategies may include word rings and semantic maps.)
- graphic tools that will help him organize and visualize information
- models of written responses

CHAPTER NINE

━━━━━━━━━

Kindergarten Reading Workshop in Action

If you are blessed to teach kindergarten in an extended-day program, you are lucky! You will have enough time in your schedule to fit in a full reading workshop and centers. If not, you will need to split up the work that occurs in reading workshop in order to fit it in the day. What is important is that children are exposed to purposeful, guided lessons that open up the joy of reading to them.

In a full kindergarten day you can run a workshop for about thirty to forty minutes prior to literacy center time. These thirty minutes would begin with a minilesson, followed by time for children to explore texts and read, and then end with a share time on the rug, when children would share their discoveries about books. If you need to break up the time to squeeze everything into a half-day schedule, you can fit a focused read-aloud into your circle time (the group meeting on the rug) and follow with time for students to explore texts. You will need both a library center where children can read for pleasure and explore books and a response-to-literature center where the children can draw or write about a recent read-aloud. Then, at the reading table you will be able to tailor instruction based on each child's conceptual development needs rather than a program that tells you day by day what to teach (McGee and Richgels 2003).

Kindergarten Interactive Read-Aloud and Comprehension

Effective instruction for kindergartners involves thoughtful interaction between the teacher and the children. While it is important to base thoughtful interaction on the individual child's needs, it is best to have a curriculum plan in place in order to teach important comprehension strategies. Young children learn to comprehend by being read to, so the read-aloud is the showcase of comprehension instruction in kindergarten. Comprehension instruction begins with the read-aloud and is reinforced by giving the children a chance to respond to literature through drawing, writing, and drama and by offering an extended time for children to explore books on their own.

The daily schedule in Chapter 2 is organized around teaching comprehension strategies during the read-aloud and during the reading workshop. Although these separate times are preferred, if you have very little wiggle room in your day, the interactive read-aloud is also effective as part of a kindergarten reading workshop. Pearson and Duke (2002) found that kindergarten children improve their comprehension of books read aloud when they focus explicitly on a comprehension strategy for an extended length of time.

Begin by telling children what the focus of the interactive read-aloud will be. After this short discussion, or a very short minilesson, read the picture book aloud, stopping to model your thinking and to use the targeted comprehension strategy. Prompt the children to talk about the text and the strategy being used and draw their attention to text features. Afterward, have the children, with a partner or in small groups, discuss using the strategy in relation to the story. For example, if the focus strategy is retelling, the children would meet with a partner or group and retell the story. After sharing orally, the children should then draw a picture or write a few sentences to retell the story.

Kindergarten Units of Study

Units of study in kindergarten need to be appropriate. While it is important to provide at-risk populations with early comprehension instruction in order to ensure they don't fall behind before entering school, it is more important that this instruction be embedded in purposeful and child-oriented classroom experiences (Tracey and Morrow 2002). These beginning units of study focus on comprehension as well as on print and the alphabetic principle. Kindergarten children need both types of instruction. Your comprehension curriculum should roll out over a school year, with a focus on a few strategies and a grand focus on a large number of read-alouds.

As children watch you and listen to you read books and discuss your thinking about books, they need to be involved in the process. You need to create teaching charts that show them your thinking and incorporate the components of the minilesson you are focusing on. By creating charts appropriate for kindergarten, you are grabbing the children's attention, tapping into visual learning, and creating purposeful and engaging print to hang in your classroom. You are also creating a powerful visual that they can refer to over and over again. In addition to helping them learn, the charts act as a reminder of what they have already learned as the charts grow in number in the classroom.

Appropriate units of study in kindergarten raise children's awareness of their thinking and thus help them develop metacognitive skills (the ability to think about their thinking). The following study units focus on the comprehension strategies young children use while they listen to books read aloud but don't overwhelm the curriculum with too great an emphasis on strategies and thinking. (They were recommended by practicing kindergarten teachers and are not meant to be a complete list.)

- *Concepts of Print*: Children become aware of print features and learn to recognize and identify print features in books and texts they encounter daily. They discuss the concepts you've chosen to focus on and locate them in picture books, big books, and leveled texts.
- *Retelling*: The focus of a retelling unit is for children to grasp story structure. Children develop the understanding that stories are told by an author; that an illustrator draws the pictures; and that stories have a beginning, a middle, and an end. They learn how to retell a story, and they may begin to realize that stories have a problem and a solution.
- *Text Connections*: Children connect to text in a personal way. They may remember something because of what is happening in the story or what they see in the illustrations. As part of the unit, children may discuss their favorite part of the story and explain why they like it.
- *Story Elements*: Children understand that stories have certain parts, including characters, settings, problems, events, and a solution (Owocki 2003). They may discuss each element, act out the story, or draw and write about the characters in the story.
- *Asking Questions*: Young children can begin to ask questions of the text as they are read to. A unit focusing on text questions can guide young children to embed their questions in something truly related to the story. Guiding children to avoid "trinket" questions like *I wonder why the girl in the picture has blue shoes?* and encouraging them to form questions about something occurring in the book like *I wonder if the wolf will eat the pigs?* helps children develop comprehension of stories read aloud.
- *Visualizing*: Teaching children to visualize as you read aloud helps them understand that reading creates pictures in our minds through language. A powerful visualization unit focuses on beautiful and descriptive language. In this unit you encourage children to focus on what they see in their minds as you read. You also encourage them to focus on how certain descriptive phrases and language develop more accurate pictures in our minds. This unit naturally folds in a focus on vocabulary and encourages young children to seek out and discuss language and words they find interesting, powerful and beautiful.

It is always difficult to decide what to teach first. While your yearlong curriculum calendar should change with the needs of your class, it does help to create a map so that you know where you are going, what your

Concepts of Print

The goal of this unit is to formally familiarize children with print so they can use text features to help them fix up their reading when they don't know a word or don't know what a sentence says. By understanding text structure and features, young children can help themselves read simple texts.

Minilessons

- *Identifying book parts*: Focus on the text features children in your class still need to learn: where to begin reading, where to go next, front and back covers, the dedication page, the table of contents.
- *Understanding punctuation*: Explicitly point out various punctuation marks in a big book and then have the children find these punctuation marks in their books.

Reading Response

Have children use sticky notes and a simple code to identify punctuation in their own books: Q (question mark), X (exclamation point), T (talking, or quotation, marks), and C (commas). Writing the code on a chart gives children something they can refer to when exploring their own books (see Figure 9.2).

A Few Good Books to Read

Any big book works well, because the print is large and the children can clearly see the periods, exclamation points, quotation marks, and other punctuation you point out. Two favorites are

- *What's the Magic Word?* by Kelly DiPucchio (2005)
- *Come Along Daisy*, by Jane Simmons (1997)

Retelling

The goal of this unit is for children to begin to understand that stories happen in a sequence and that if they remember the sequence, they can remember the story. Each suggested minilesson may last more than one day.

Minilessons

- *How to tell what a story is about*: Explicitly show and model how to retell a story.
- *What do I think of the story?* Think aloud about whether you like or don't like a story and why.
- *Stories have a beginning, middle, and end*: Explain that stories have a predictable order. Tell children that they can "talk across their fingers"—that is, use their fingers to help remember the sequence of events.

FIGURE 9.2 Teaching Chart About Identifying Punctuation

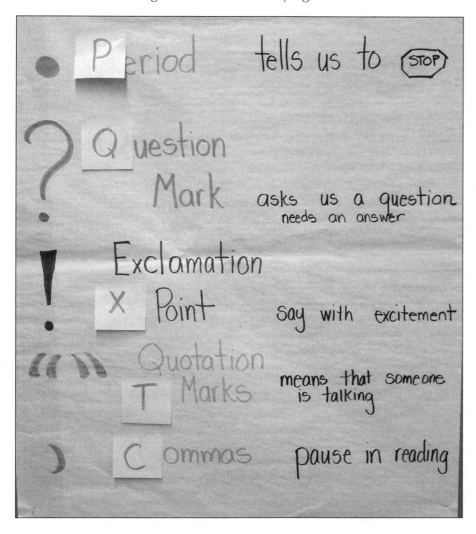

- *Rethinking a book is retelling a book*: While retelling a story, stop and share your thinking aloud.
- *Say it quick: summarize important stuff*: Show children how to retell without giving too many details.
- *Share a retelling with a partner*: Model how to retell a story to one other person; emphasize that long retellings are boring and your partner might fall asleep! Emphasize talking across their fingers to remember story events.
- *Writing a retelling*: Model how to retell a story on paper. (See the appendix, page 180, for a sample retelling response form.)

A Few Good Books to Read

- *Rosie's Roses*, by Pamela Duncan Edwards (2003)
- *Julius, the Baby of the World*, by Kevin Henkes (1995)
- *Owen*, by Kevin Henkes (1993b)
- *Rosy's Visitors*, by Judy Hindley (2002)

Text Connections

This unit focuses on helping children connect with text by thinking of things they know or are interested in that relate to events or characters in the story. They may relate to their personal experiences (text to self), to other books they know (text to text), or to things they know about the world (text to world). Kindergartners love to share parts of a story that they find funny, interesting, silly, or touching or that remind them of something from their lives.

Minilessons

- *What does the story remind you of?* Show children how you think about connections while reading. Encourage them to think of things that the book reminds them of. Do this with many different picture books and texts over time.
- *What is a text-to-self connection?* When we are reading and remember something that happened to us that is similar to what is happening in the story, we are making a text-to-self connection. Encourage children to make connections and share those connections with a partner.
- *Remembering other books we have read and how they go together*: Explain that when we are reading or listening to a story and remember another story we know, we are making a text-to-text connection. Think aloud as you make a text-to-text connection while reading.
- *What do you know about the world that reminds you of the story?* Remind the children that they've already made text-to-self and text-to-text connections. Tell them that when they are reading or listening to a story and they think about something they know about the world, they are making a text-to-world connection.
- *Sharing a favorite part*: Show children your favorite part in a book. Tell them how identifying your favorite part helps you connect to the book. Explicitly show children how to write and draw a text-to-self connection based on their favorite part. Encourage them to put all their ideas on the page, in the drawing or the writing or both. Have children share their written response with a partner. (See Figure A–3 in the Appendix, page 179, for a sample text-connection response form.)

Reading Response

Figure 9.3 shows Ayeshia's response to *Julius, the Baby of the World*, by Kevin Henkes. Ayeshia writes, *The sister reminds me of when I was jealous of*

FIGURE 9.3 Ayeshia's Text-to-Self Connection

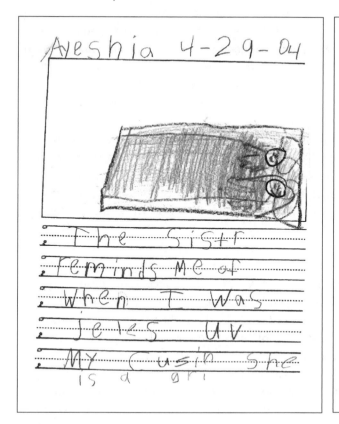

Ayeshia 4-29-04

The Sistr reminds Me of When I was jeles uv My cusin she is a girl

and hur Naym is Slest But I got Yoosf To hur a lot I love hr A lot because she is cyowt a lot,

my cousin. She is a girl and her name is Celeste. But I got used to her a lot. I love
her a lot because she is cute a lot.

A Few Good Books to Read

- *Toot and Puddle: The New Friend*, by Hollie Hobbie (2003b)
- *Toot and Puddle: Charming Opal*, by Hollie Hobbie (2003a)
- *Sometimes I'm Bombaloo*, by Rachel Vail (2005)
- *The Ticky Tacky Doll*, by Cynthia Rylant (2002)
- *Max Cleans Up*, by Rosemary Wells (2000)
- *On the Beach*, by Alastair Smith and Laura Howell (2004) (This is part of the Lift-the-Flap Book series, published by Usborne Books, which is a wonderful way for young children to explore nonfiction.)

Story Elements

The goal of this unit is for children to begin to understand that stories have certain features. These story elements help their comprehension. The children can focus on the beginning, middle, and end of the story in their retellings.

Minilessons

- *What are the story elements?* Explain what story elements are and tell children how these story elements help you understand what you are reading. Kindergartners can easily understand setting, character, and problem and solution (the plot). Post teaching charts that depict story elements graphically. (Figure 9.4 shows a bulletin board based on story elements. Figure 9.5 shows a teaching chart from a minilesson describing story elements.)

- *How story elements help us understand what we read*: While reading aloud, discuss your thinking. Tell children what you notice (who the characters are) and what you think is happening in the story (problem and solution).

- *Identifying characters*: Talk about the characters in books you have read aloud. Do this many times with many books. Have the children identify the characters.

- *Identifying the setting*: Talk about the setting in books you have read aloud. Help the children see the connection between the setting and your understanding of the book: "If the story takes place in the mountains, I know there will be trees and hills and the weather will be colder."

- *Identifying the problem and solution*: Talk about the plot in various books. Explain that the plot is the problem in the story and the solution that happens near the end.

- *Retelling stories, focusing on the beginning, middle, and end*: During a retelling, model for children how you remember the story elements. Talk about the beginning and the characters and setting, then move to the middle and the developing problem, then describe the end when the problem is resolved.

FIGURE 9.4 Story Element Board

FIGURE 9.5 Story Element Chart Focusing on Characters

Reading Response

In Zelicious' response to *A Baby Sister for Frances*, by Russell Hoban (1976; see Figure 9.6), she chooses a favorite character: *My favorite character is Gloria the baby. She is sweet when she is asleep because she is quiet with her baby.*

A Few Good Books to Read

- *Olivia*, by Ian Falconer (2000)
- *Elena's Serenade*, by Campbell Geeslin (2004)
- *Chyrsanthemum*, by Kevin Henkes (1996a)
- *Lily's Purple Plastic Purse*, by Kevin Henkes (1996b)
- *Poodlena*, by E. B. McHenry (2004)
- *The Old Man and His Door*, by Gary Soto (1996)

Asking Questions

Young children need to learn to ask questions of the text in order to monitor their own comprehension. They need to stop from time to time and think about what they have read. This is facilitated by "I wonder why . . ." questions. Young children should have the opportunity to think like this during read-alouds.

Minilessons

- *Why good readers ask questions of the text*: Discuss how readers ask questions in order to understand what they read. (A sample teaching chart that directs children's attention to their thinking while reading or listening to a story is shown in Figure 9.7.)

FIGURE 9.6 Zelicious' Response About a Favorite Character

- *How to ask right-there and deep questions*: Help children understand the differences between *right-there*, or surface, questions and *deep* questions that get at what things mean. Young children tend to ask questions that don't pertain to the story; guide them to think about the story and wonder what is happening and why.
- *Wondering about the characters*: Model how you wonder about a character's thoughts, actions, or feelings. Focus on the language you use: "I wonder why . . . ," "I wonder if . . ."
- *Wondering about the problem and solution*: Ask questions aloud when reading about the problem in the story, and then model questions that help you predict the solution to the problem.

Reading Response

Figure 9.8 shows Zelicious' "I wonder" question about the character Owen and his beloved blanket in Kevin Henkes' *Owen* (1993b): *I wonder why Owen was taking his blanket everywhere and it was dirty but his mom said it is OK.* She wrote this piece in April, when she had learned a lot about reading and

FIGURE 9.7 Teaching Chart on Questioning a Text

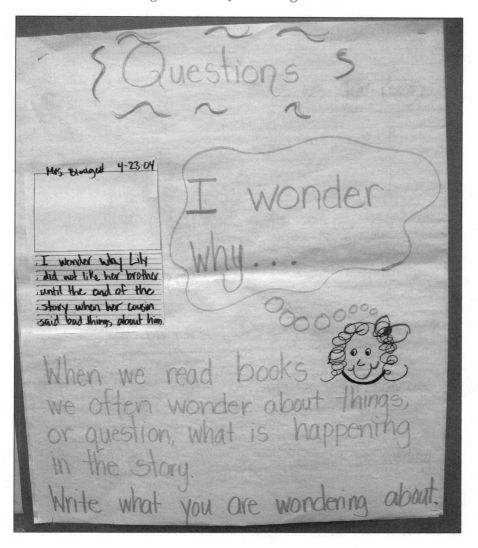

how to respond to a book. She was able to focus on one part of the book, write a sentence about this character, and then draw a picture that matched her writing.

A Few Good Books to Read

- *Moonbear's Skyfire*, by Frank Asch (1999)
- *Pinduli*, by Janell Cannon (2004)
- *Don't Need Friends*, by Carolyn Crimi (2000)
- *Goldie Locks Has Chicken Pox*, by Erin Dealey (2002)
- *Hunter's Best Friend at School*, by Laura Malone Elliot (2002)
- *Bunny Cakes*, by Rosemary Wells (1997)

FIGURE 9.8 Zelicious' "I Wonder" Question

Visualizing

It is important for young children to pay attention to their thinking. They need to know that readers see images while reading. The focus of this unit is on developing children's skill in seeing the images being described in the text. In addition to discussing what they see, children can reenact the story, therefore making the story visible.

Minilessons

■ *What do you see in your mind when I read to you?* Tell the children to close their eyes while you read and to focus on what they see in their imaginations. Help them understand that words create images in our minds.

■ *How the words make us feel*: Help children understand that good readers not only see things in their minds but feel things as well. Share your feelings about something that occurs in a book you are reading—do you feel sorry, sad, happy, angry?

- *Finding and recording descriptive language*: Explore beautiful and descriptive phrases and words in books. Single these out and discuss them. Talk about how descriptive language helps you visualize while reading. Display beautiful words on a bulletin board or in a pocket chart.

A Few Good Books to Read

- *Names for Snow*, by Judi K. Beach (2003)
- *Snog the Frog*, by Tony Bonning (2004)
- *Fishing in the Air*, by Sharon Creech (2000)
- *Hello, Harvest Moon*, by Ralph Fletcher (2003)
- *Little Dog and Duncan*, by Kristine O'Connell George (2002)
- *If Kisses Were Colors*, by Janet Lawler (2003)
- *Snow Music*, by Lynne Rae Perkins (2003)
- *Won't You Be My Kissaroo?* by Joanne Ryder (2004)
- *Scarecrow*, by Cynthia Rylant (1998)
- *The Stars Will Shine*, by Cynthia Rylant (2005)

Classroom Essentials: Supporting Reading Workshop in Kindergarten

You can support the youngest readers by ensuring that classroom features scaffold their emerging literacy consciousness. Features that are essential to supporting your units of study and that will help you successfully roll out reading workshop in your kindergarten classroom include

- *A library or book corner*: An area where children can explore books and other texts during literacy centers.
- *Simple homemade books*: A resource for free-reading time at school and at home. You can create these simple books on a computer. Choose a repetitive text structure like "I can see" or "I like." Finish each sentence with words that match what you have been studying: "I like school. I like reading. I like playing." On a computer, type out one line of text for each half page. Print, cut the pages in half, staple, and voila!—a book. (Have children draw illustrations or use clip art.) Children can practice reading these simple stories at the reading table or at home and work with sentences and words from them in a pocket chart. After they are very familiar with the stories, they can store them in their book boxes.
- *Response-to-literature station*: A center where children can respond to a favorite book or a recent read-aloud. (See the example in Figure 9.9.)
- *Interactive word wall*: A pocket chart or wall area filled with words and small library pockets stapled next to the words. The library pockets are filled with small cards containing the words that the children can carry to their work area when writing. The interactive word wall can include

FIGURE 9.9 A Response-to-Literature Station

beautiful words, sight words, favorite phrases from storybooks, terms from favorite nonfiction sources, and other words essential to the children in your classroom, depending on their interest in specific books or content.

CHAPTER TEN

First-Grade Reading Workshop in Action

Just before I sat down to write this chapter, a colleague asked for my help in designing her first-grade classroom. She pleaded, "When I *see* something, I understand how to do it in my room with my kids. Please help!" Her comment reminded me that some teachers need a visual guide to how the reading workshop *looks* each day—how the walls look and change with each unit of study and how children's writing about reading looks as it develops over time. Therefore, I've turned this chapter and Chapter 11 into "picture books," set up to guide and sharpen your vision of comprehension instruction in the primary reading workshop. (Reading response frames designed to support first graders as they think and write about texts are included in the appendix.)

Focused Instruction for First Graders

Kristina Karlson is a first-grade teacher at Pinedale Elementary School. Children cannot help but learn in her classroom; it is the site of excellent teaching, an exemplar of how to immerse children in print and how to scaffold children who need support in learning how to read.

Kristina's room drips with language, language supports, and appropriate expectations. Her students are learning in a carefully constructed classroom based on the research of Tracey and Morrow (2002):

- It is integrated.
- It uses theme-based reading strategies.
- It is literature based.
- It is focused on developing comprehension.
- It uses a balance of impromptu teaching moments and carefully structured instruction.

- It includes explicit skill instruction.
- It is set up to encourage collaboration.
- It develops highly motivated children.

In addition to using well-organized units of study, Kristina implements three instructional components in her classroom:

- She provides reading spaces.
- She has children work with words.
- She creates walls that teach.

Reading space is important. When children know they have a predictable and particular place to go during reading workshop, they can settle in and concentrate quickly. If young children are to develop the stamina to read for thirty continuous minutes, they need space to wiggle, jostle, and stretch without bothering anyone.

What children read is also important. Kristina's classroom doesn't have many bookcases, so she organizes her books in baskets placed around the room. The baskets are easy to reach, and children select their own books during each day's book switch, which takes place first thing in the morning. Kristina doesn't want the children wandering around the room when they should be getting a lot of reading done!

Word work needs to be prominent throughout the day. Kristina records students' words, word families, and spelling patterns on charts that flood the room and support children when they are working independently.

Kristina also creates walls that teach (Akhavan 2004). The information on the walls stands in for Kristina when she is not working directly with a child. Think of the teaching charts in your room. Consider how they support learning:

- What can the children remember from instruction?
- What will they attempt with the help of prompts they see on a wall chart?
- What can they do on their own?

Special Reading Places

The children in Kristina's classroom are independent learners focused on practicing what Kristina teaches daily in the minilesson. They read each day in their special spots in the classroom and they respond orally and in writing. It is hard to imagine what this may look like as the children leave the carpet area and find a place to read. Often when I step into Kristina's room, children are scattered about everywhere, reading. She doesn't have classroom management problems during the workshop because the children highly value their special sitting spots and know that they are a privilege. Their desks wait as a second alternative. Notice in Figures 10.1, 10.2, and 10.3 how it looks when the children are spread around the room. Their books are laid out in an organized fashion and the book boxes are close by.

FIGURE 10.1 Children Read and Share as a Whole Group

FIGURE 10.2 Children Read from Book Boxes in Kristina's Classroom

FIGURE 10.3 One Child Reading with Her Books Organized Around Her

Word Work

Kristina's word work charts ensure that the children have a visual reminder of previous phonics and spelling lessons. These charts help them recall and use the information on their own. The chart in Figure 10.4 lists the steps children should take when they come to a word they don't know. The chart in Figure 10.5 presents the family of words that contain a silent *e*.

Walls That Teach

What is important should get written down: *if you think it, ink it*. When children can see what they have been told orally, they learn much faster. Young children need to be immersed in the language of the classroom, so Kristina focuses on making the language and the thinking behind it transparent. The charts on her walls are a way to help children remember; for example, the chart in Figure 10.6 reminds students of the reading workshop routine. There is no reason that information should be presented only orally. When we tap children's visual way of knowing—if we fill the walls with instruction—they are learning. When the children look at the charts, they

FIGURE 10.4 Kristina's Chart on Fix-Up Steps

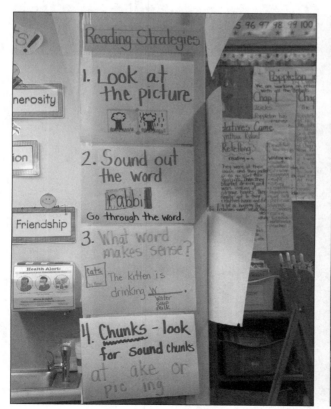

FIGURE 10.5 Word Work Chart

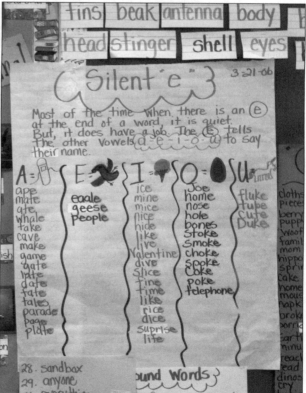

FIGURE 10.6 Kristina's Chart Helps Children Visualize Their Tasks During Reading Workshop

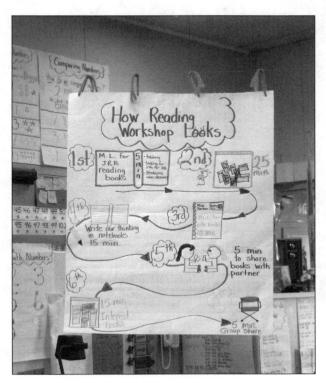

remind themselves of what to do, what to focus on, and what is important. Classroom walls filled with visuals focused on the real work of reading and writing begin to teach after a minilesson is over.

Each chart focuses on a single strategy. This helps children develop a metacognitive awareness of comprehension strategies and how they help the reader understand what the words in a text are saying. But Kristina also encourages children to use more than one strategy at a time.

The charts in Figures 10.7 through 10.10 are a few examples of how charts help guide students' thinking. Figure 10.7 shows children how to record reading responses in their notebooks. The four-block chart in Figure 10.8 helps children record story elements. Figure 10.9 contains examples of right-there, or skinny, questions and deep, or fat, questions. The chart in Figure 10.10 was created when children thought of their own fat and skinny questions, wrote the questions on sticky notes, and placed them on the chart.

FIGURE 10.7 Chart on How to Use a Reading Notebook

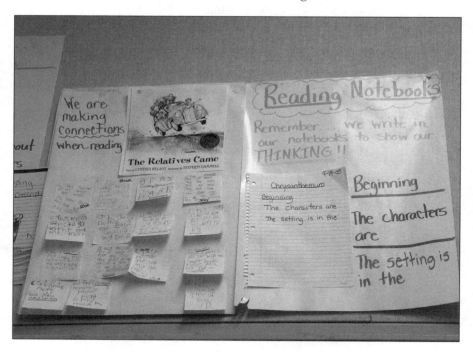

FIGURE 10.8 Chart on How to Analyze Story Elements

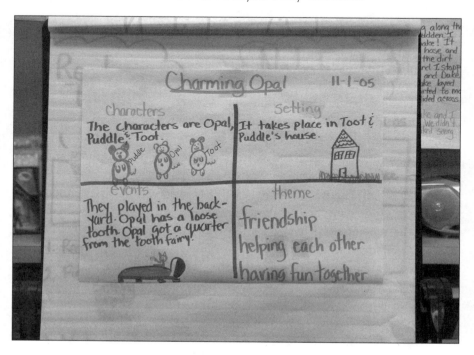

FIGURE 10.9 Chart Demonstrating Teacher Thinking on Fat and Skinny Questions

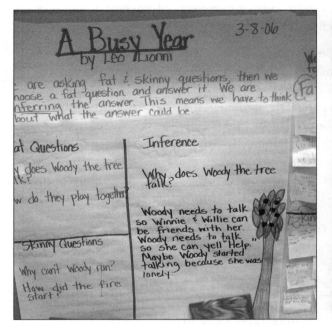

FIGURE 10.10 Chart of Children's Fat and Skinny Questions

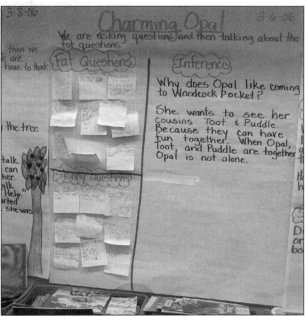

First-Grade Units of Study

The comprehension strategies taught in first grade are the same as those taught in kindergarten. However, in first grade the goal is for children to apply the strategies independently to grade-level text. In addition to thinking independently, the children write more as a way to learn to think. First graders are also often ready to focus on additional fix-up or comprehension strategies. You can plan your yearlong curriculum using the units described in Chapter 9 but layer in support for children to work independently. You might also consider these additional units of study:

- *Identifying a Purpose for Reading*: Children develop an understanding of the reading-writing connection. They write their ideas about their reading for others to enjoy and understand. They identify a reason to read and then focus on that objective while reading: "Today I will write a text-to-self connection I made when reading a book in my book box."
- *Creating Our Reading Room*: Children learn how to spend time actually reading. They read routinely in a wide variety of texts and genres. They discuss new ideas and focus on understanding new vocabulary and concepts. Overall they become a reading community.
- *Making Deeper Text Connections*: Children first summarize in order to be able to describe their connection in detail. They learn to think about a character's actions, thoughts, and feelings and the ideas presented in nonfiction texts.

- *Recognizing Nonfiction Text Structures*: Children begin to see the differences between story elements and nonfiction elements. They identify nonfiction features of print and begin to glean information from these text structures as well as from the text.

The reading work in first grade becomes more intense as the year goes on, but often teachers ask, "How do I get started?" Kristina rolls out her reading workshop in September and October. By the end of October her goal is for the children to be independent in the workshop and ready to focus on comprehension strategies. Her first unit is "Developing Our Reading Life" (see the plan in Figure 10.11). She begins the year by having children explore a large number of books and find characters with whom they connect. During this unit Kristina replaces guided reading instruction with DRA assessments of each child's reading ability or reading readiness.

FIGURE 10.11 Plan for "Developing Our Reading Life" Unit

First-Grade Reading Workshop—September

Sample Minilessons for Launch Unit

1. Introduce the reading workshop and share a favorite book.
2. Introduce book boxes and show children how to self-select texts.
3. Introduce notebooks/folders and how to use them. Show where response paper is kept in the classroom.
4. Review yesterday's lesson and model using a student sample. Is the response in the folder? Are the children finding a special spot to sit in the room? Are they keeping track of their book box?
5. Introduce how to partner share; review rules; model; and practice.
6. Review partner share and practice.
7. Introduce how to group share. Let each child share at the end of the workshop.
8. Building stamina: Are the children reading for fifteen minutes or longer? Add a little bit of time to the clock each day.
9. Strategy: What to do when you are distracted from your reading— Look at the pictures or reread.
10. Review yesterday's lesson and have children share what they do to keep themselves on track.
11. Strategy: What to do when you are stuck on a word. How to chunk words and get your brain ready for the first sound.
12. Review strategy conversation with students. Model thinking aloud for the class; write the ideas on a chart.
13. Introduce character as a story element.
14. Describe characters' physical characteristics. Use pictures.
15. Describe character thoughts and actions. "What do you think the character is thinking?" Write the character thoughts in a response.

FIGURE 10.12 Plan for "Being a Good Reader" Unit

First-Grade Reading Workshop—October

Sample Minilessons for "Being a Good Reader" Unit

1. Introduce concept of how to be a good reader.
2. Repeat yesterday's lesson and add "getting our minds ready to read." Discuss what students should think about when reading.
3. Introduce how to make predictions. Tell children that good readers make predictions about the book before and during reading.
4. Review the concepts of getting ready to read and making predictions.
5. Celebrate reading: Have each student share a book. Have the children shop for new books to fill their book boxes.
6. Strategy: What to do when stuck on a word—Introduce how to look at the picture for a clue about word meaning.
7. Review yesterday's lesson.
8. Show children what it looks like when they confer and discuss the conferring schedule.
9. Review conferring and confer with one group after guided reading.
10. Strategy: What to do when stuck on a word—Think about what would make sense in the sentence.
11. Strategy: What to do when stuck on a word—Sound out the word, looking at the letters and blending.
12. Strategy: What to do when stuck on a word—Read through the whole word, looking at all the letters and sounding them out.
13. Strategy: What to do when stuck on a word—Read through the whole word, think about what the word says, put the letters together for sounds.
14. Celebrate reading: Have each student share a book. Have the children shop for new books to fill their book boxes.
15. Explain that readers always think about what makes sense.
16. Strategy: What to do when stuck on a word—Think about the picture and think about what is happening in the book. Ask, "What would make sense?"
17. Tell children to persevere—good readers keep trying.

Kristina's next unit is "Being a Good Reader" (see the plan in Figure 10.12). Children focus on using fix-up strategies to help them figure out and decode unknown words, fluency to help them read with automaticity, and on becoming a community of readers that guide, help, and teach one another and celebrate books together.

Student Growth in Reading Response Over Time

First graders' ability to respond to texts will develop over time. You can use the response frames in the appendix to help your students become independent during the workshop. They can choose the response frame they need depending on the text they have read or on the focus of your minilesson.

Figure 10.13 is a response written by Kimbra in April. Kimbra was no longer using response frames but was instead writing her responses in a booklet of lined paper (with space for a picture) stapled together. Kimbra had listened to *The Pain and the Great One* (Blume 1985) a few days before and was very interested in the story. Kimbra's text-to-self connection shows that she understood how to respond to text: *Today I read The Pain and the Great One. It reminds me about my sister. She gets more attention than me because she is little. I get jealous of her. But sometimes I get agreeing with her.*

Some students do need the support of the writing frames. Over time they should be able to respond without using a frame or use more sophisticated frames that prompt deeper thinking. The samples in Figures 10.14 through 10.19, all written after she read just-right books, show Emily's writing and

FIGURE 10.13 Kimbra's Text-to-Self Connection, Written in the Spring

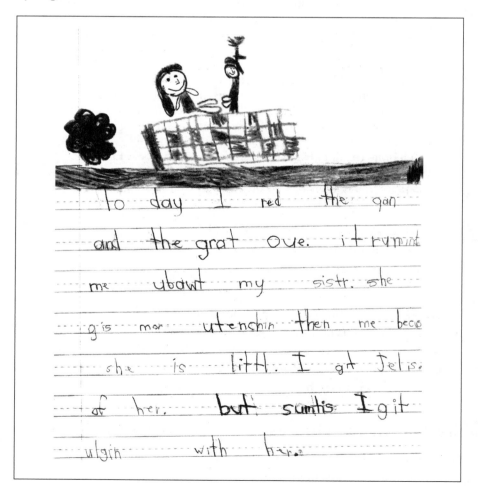

growth over time. Figure 10.14 is from the first week of first grade; Figure 10.19 is from early in February. Notice how Emily's thinking and ability to respond change and develop. The progression of the units of study is also evident: text connections, favorite part, character analysis, story elements, and visualization (mental pictures).

FIGURE 10.14 Emily's Book Response from the First Week of School

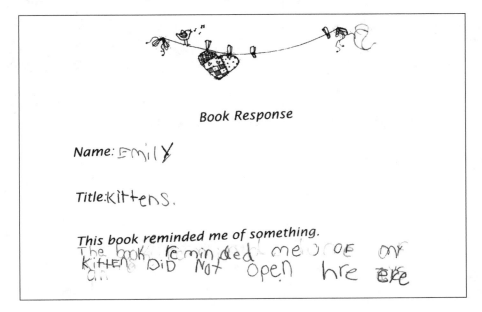

FIGURE 10.15 Emily's Text Connection

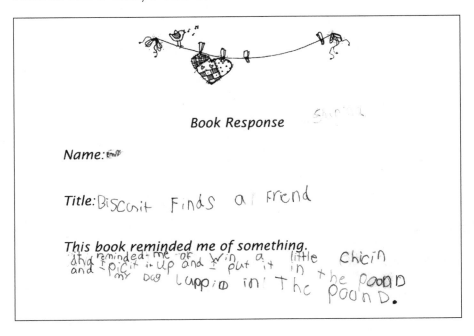

FIGURE 10.16 Emily's Favorite-Part
Response

Book Response

Name: Emily

Title: IFF You Give a PiG a PaNcaKe

Let me tell you about my favorite part.

My favorite part is whin
She get in the Bath
BuBuls are BiG
She mit grawn BiG
IF I was hr
I WuD br q DiE
Ticki q mrmalb

FIGURE 10.17 Emily's Character
Analysis

Book Response

Name: Emily.

Title: mother hippoptamus's dry Skin.

Let me tell you about a character in the book.

The character in the book
was happy beCause mother hippuptamuss
pap the mad on hr!

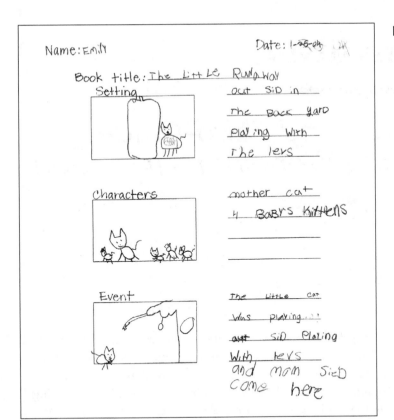

FIGURE 10.18 Emily's Story Analysis

Name: Emily   Date: 1-26-04

Book title: The Little Runaway

Setting

out sid in
the Back yard
Playing With
The lers

Characters

mother cat
4 BaBrs Kittens

Event

The Little cat
was playing
out sid Playing
With kevs
and mom sied
come here

FIGURE 10.19 Emily's Mental-Pictures Response

Book Response

Name: Emily

Title: Bread

I was making mental pictures when I read.

I can see... me and my brother
Wit to The Bread Store
on The way Back
We seen a haigring Dog
We seen a haigring Ducks
my mom sane to me
Wer is The rist
of The Bread
my mom sane
to me my
Dad sane
hear it is.
the Ean

CHAPTER ELEVEN

Second- and Third-Grade Reading Workshops in Action

The units of study presented in this chapter are appropriate for second and third grades. While some of them overlap units in lower grade levels, the difference is in the rigor of the work. For example, third graders apply comprehension strategies while reading more difficult books and their reading responses are longer and more in depth. All of the units focus on giving children strategies that they can then use independently—essentially, loading up their strategy backpacks. By reading a lot and often, by participating in clear minilessons focused on one objective, by writing to process thinking and comprehension, children own the skills they need to become fluent, independent readers.

You can make the greatest impact in your second- or third-grade classroom by focusing on student learning. The children need to know what they are learning and why. Therefore, strategy instruction in the second and third grades is more direct and focused:

- This is the concept/strategy we are going to learn today.
- This is how I want you to think about this concept/strategy.
- Watch how I apply the strategy when I am reading.
- Now you're going to do what I just did while you are reading independently.
- Then I want you to write about your reading in order to think clearly about what you tried to do.

Although these units of study are not specific to grade-level standards for any particular state or area, their outcomes or goals are based on standards documents. Any unit can be easily adapted to a related goal or standard in your state guidelines, thus allowing you to meet your district's expectations and maintain a rigorous program.

What's in This Chapter?

These units of study were created by Hollie Olsen and Pam Pflepsen at Pinedale Elementary School. (See Chapters 2 and 4 for more about these teachers' work.) The units are

- Identifying a Favorite Part (Identifying a Purpose for Reading)
- Retelling
- Making Text-to-Self Connections
- Making Text-to-Text Connections
- Making Text-to-World Connections
- Identifying Text Structure
- Comparing and Contrasting Text Structures

You needn't use all of them or follow this sequence.

Each unit of study is discussed separately. The basic unit map for each is presented as a three- or four-week calendar listing the objective, or focus, of each day's minilesson (with some days devoted to sharing student responses). Also included are examples of teaching charts to support student learning, teaching tips (for some units), and examples of students' written responses using response frames. The writing samples will help you understand the outcome of each unit, but your students may be able to write with more creativity and detail. (Third graders often don't use response frames; the samples of third-grade writing provided here were generated without the use of frames.) A list of response frames is on p. 178.

Unit 1

Identifying a Favorite Part

In this unit, students read for enjoyment and practice as they identify their favorite part and share it. The focus is on

- how reading workshop works every day
- reading with a purpose
- responding to literature with a response frame or in a journal
- how the minilesson works (*My job is to think, listen, do.*)
- how to use a book box and choose interesting and just-right books

Figure 11.1 is the map for this unit; Figures 11.2 through 11.6 are some teaching charts from the unit; and Figures 11.7 and 11.8 are samples of student work produced during the unit. The favorite part response frames are found on pp. 179, 181, 182, and 207.

FIGURE 11.1 Plan for "Identifying a Favorite Part" Unit

Reading Workshop Three-Week Minilesson Map
Unit of Study: Identifying a Favorite Part

Unit 1

	Monday	Tuesday	Wednesday	Thursday	Friday
	Introduce chart and model response Focus on favorite part	Share student examples and teacher model for bulletin board	Review sticky notes procedure Teach how to identify favorite part	Review how to choose just-right books	
	Teach "What Do Good Readers Do?" chart	Share student examples of favorite part response writing	Discuss what makes a section a favorite part. Discuss thinking about our reading		Share a new teacher model, expanding with details
	Teach expanding our responses with our thinking	Share student examples. What makes them good responses?	Review choosing just-right books		

Some days are intentionally left blank so they can be filled in as unit of study develops, based on students' needs.

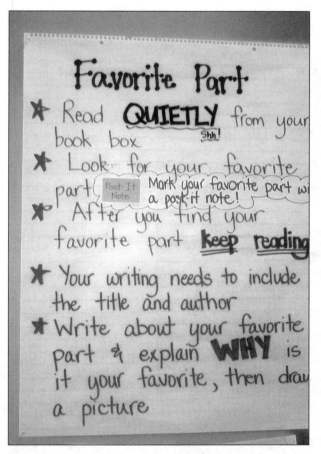

FIGURE 11.2

A few teaching charts that guide student thinking during the "Favorite Part" unit (the first unit of the year) include 11.3, Books that are in the book box, and 11.2, How to respond in writing about your favorite part.

FIGURE 11.3

FIGURE 11.4

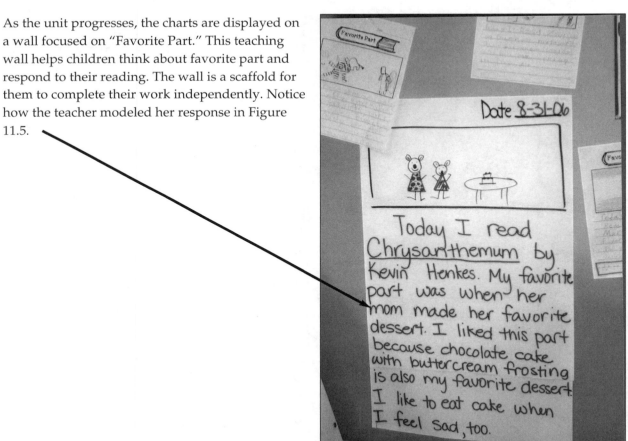

FIGURE 11.5

As the unit progresses, the charts are displayed on a wall focused on "Favorite Part." This teaching wall helps children think about favorite part and respond to their reading. The wall is a scaffold for them to complete their work independently. Notice how the teacher modeled her response in Figure 11.5.

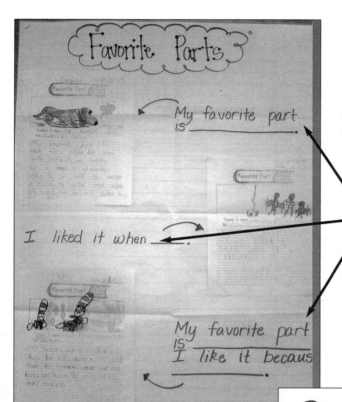

FIGURE 11.6A

During this unit of study, children focus on how to identify a favorite part in a story. The response frames give the children a kick start and a safety net to begin writing their response (Figure 11.6B).

FIGURE 11.6B

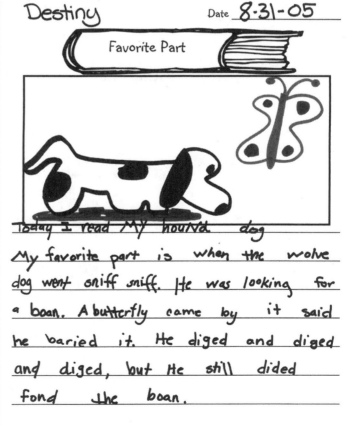

Destiny   Date 8-31-05

Favorite Part

Today I read My hourld dog
My favorite part is when the wolve
dog went sniff sniff. He was looking for
a boan. A butterfly came by it said
he baried it. He diged and diged
and diged, but He still dided
fond the boan.

FIGURE 11.7 Second-Grade Writing Sample: Identifying a Favorite Part

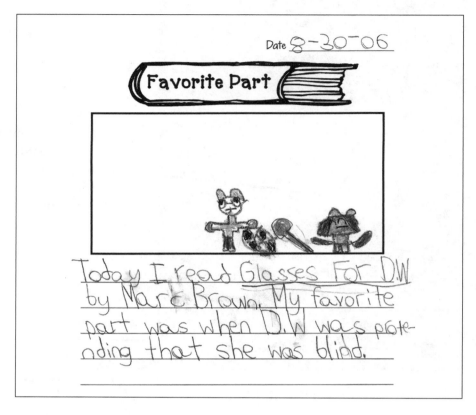

Date 8-30-06

Favorite Part

Today I read Glasses For DW by Marc Brown. My favorite part was when D.W was pretending that she was blind.

FIGURE 11.8 Third-Grade Writing Sample: Identifying a Favorite Part

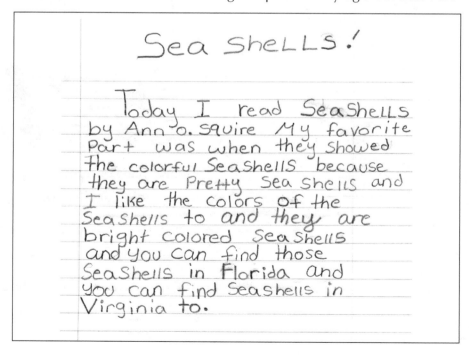

Sea SHeLLS!

Today I read SeaShells by Ann o. squire My favorite Part was when they showed the colorful Seashells because they are Pretty Sea shells and I like the colors of the Seashells to and they are bright colored Sea Shells and you can find those Seashells in Florida and you can find Seashells in Virginia to.

Unit 2

Retelling

In this unit, students read a story independently, record important parts of the story (beginning, middle, and end) on sticky notes, and attach the sticky notes to a response frame. (The retelling response frame is included in the Appendix on pages 188, 192.) The focus is on

■ using sticky notes to record thinking and stay focused
■ identifying the important parts of the text
■ moving from retelling to summarizing
■ identifying the main idea and details when summarizing

Figure 11.9 is the map for this unit; Figures 11.10 through 11.13 show some teaching charts from the unit; and Figure 11.14 is a sample of student work produced during the unit.

Hollie and Pam's Teaching Tips

- We teach this unit at the beginning of the year because children are learning to choose just-right books that require them to use reading strategies but that aren't so difficult they get stuck. The focus is narrow: choosing just-right books, reading with a purpose (reading to retell), and starting response journals.
- The basic story structure we teach is beginning, middle, and end. We want children to think of the retelling as a summary—a short, focused response.
- We model using strategies that focus on retelling.
- We make sure that we use literature that is beautiful and engaging.

FIGURE 11.9 Plan for "Retelling" Unit

Reading Workshop Four-Week Minilesson Map
Unit of Study: Retelling

Unit 2

Monday	Tuesday	Wednesday	Thursday	Friday
Introduce teaching chart and model retelling	Teach sticky notes procedure	Share student examples of a simple retelling and teacher model for bulletin board	Discuss what is in a good retelling. Highlight main characters	
What is in a good retelling? Highlight setting	Share student examples of retelling that include character and setting	What is in a good retelling? Highlight beginning	What is in a good retelling? Highlight middle	
What is in a good retelling? Highlight end	Introduce "What Do Good Readers Do?" chart. Share how good readers retell	What is in a good retelling? Highlight problem and solution		How are we using our precious reading time? Refocus readers
Model how to add important parts to retelling responses	Review main character and setting	Review beginning, middle, and end		

Some days are intentionally left blank so they can be filled in as unit of study develops, based on students' needs.

FIGURE 11.10

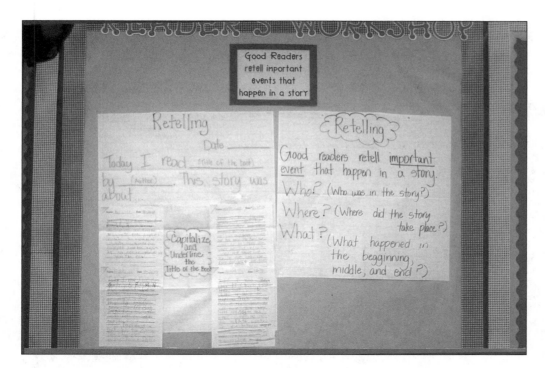

Teaching charts are used during the direct instruction portion of the minilesson and model teacher thinking. These charts are visual models for children that they refer to often while working independently. Figure 11.10 includes charts with teacher thinking and student work samples.

FIGURE 11.11

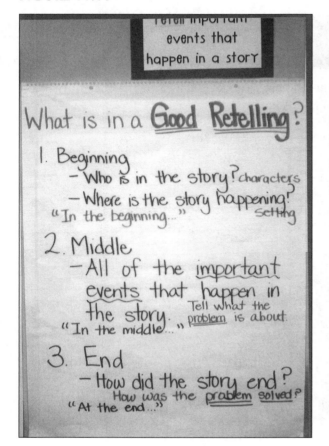

FIGURE 11.12

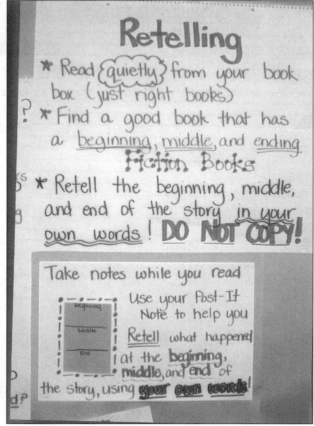

The children are encouraged to think through *how* to do the work during the minilesson. Notice how explicit the information is in the charts in Figures 11.11 and 11.12. These charts explain, model, and reinforce purposeful thinking.

FIGURE 11.13

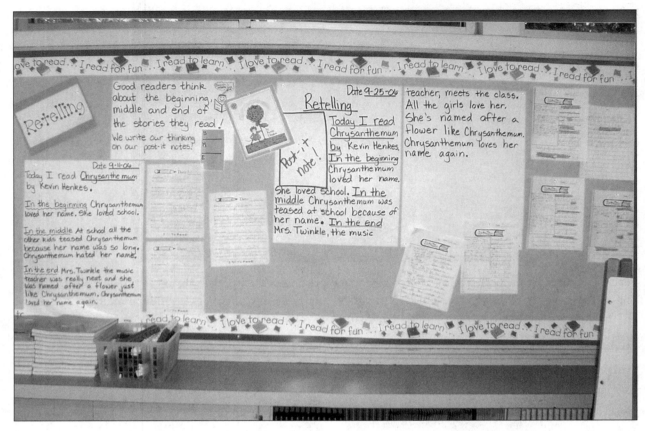

Figure 11.13 is an example of a teaching wall for the retelling unit. This wall developed over time as each minilesson was taught, work was celebrated, and thinking was shared.

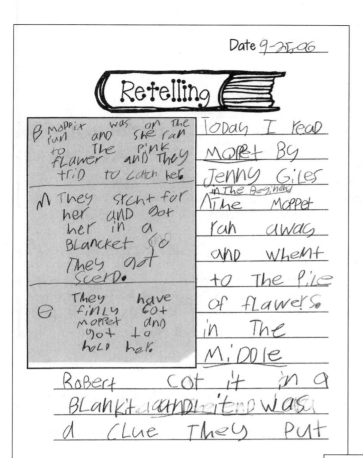

Date 9-25-06

Retelling

B Moppit was on the run and she ran to the pink flawer and they trid to catch her.

M They srcht for her and got her in a Blancket so they got scerd.

E They have finly got moppet and got to hold her.

Today I read Moppet By Jenny Giles in The Begining The Moppet ran away, and whent to the pile of flawers. in the middle Robert cot it in a Blankit and it was a clue they put

FIGURE 11.14 Writing Sample: Retelling

The Blankit on a pile of leves. in the end Lara got to hold Moppit it was happy.

Unit 3

Making Text-to-Self Connections

In this unit, students identify something in a book that reminds them of something they know or something from their life. They jot the connection on a sticky note and attach it to the corresponding page in the book. The focus is on

- connecting to characters' feelings
- identifying with events or character actions
- providing a three-part response: book title, page where connection was made, and description of connection
- placing the sticky note on the page of the book where the connection was made
- referring back to the sticky note to jog thinking

Figure 11.15 is the map for this unit; Figures 11.16 through 11.18 show some teaching charts from the unit; and Figure 11.19 is a sample of student work produced during the unit. Text-to-Self Response Frames are on pp. 183, 193, and 194.

FIGURE 11.15 Plan for "Making Text-to-Self Connections" Unit

Unit 3

Reading Workshop Four-Week Minilesson Map
Unit of Study: Making Text-to-Self Connections

Monday	Tuesday	Wednesday	Thursday	Friday
Introduce teaching chart and model response	Review sticky notes procedure for making text-to-self connections	Share student examples and teacher model for wall	Focus on sticky notes and share student examples	Review what a connection is
Model how to expand thinking Teach students to focus on deeper connections	Model how to generate alternate ways to write "this reminds me of . . ."	Review model Up to this point they are only writing on sticky notes	Introduce response sheet Focus on extended writing format—introduce new teaching chart	Focus on part 1 of response sheet "Today I read _____"
Share student examples of part 1	Focus on part 2 of response sheet "In the story . . ."	Share student examples of part 2	Focus on part 3 of response sheet "This reminds me of . . ."	Share student examples of part 3
Model how to add details to our connections	Model how to make it come alive in your reader's mind		Review parts 1–3 of response sheet with details	

Some days are intentionally left blank so they can be filled in as unit of study develops, based on students' needs.

The teaching chart in Figure 11.16 is one of the first examples given to the class.

In Figure 11.17, notice how the teacher models the thinking on a large chart.

Later during the unit, she models the thinking on the same paper the students will use to write their responses. The teacher carefully models how to use a sticky note to jot a note during the workshop. After jotting down their ideas, the children place the sticky note on the edge of the page and continue reading from their book boxes. Then, when it is time to write, they place the sticky note on the responses sheet and write their response using the sticky note to jog their memory.

FIGURE 11.16

FIGURE 11.17

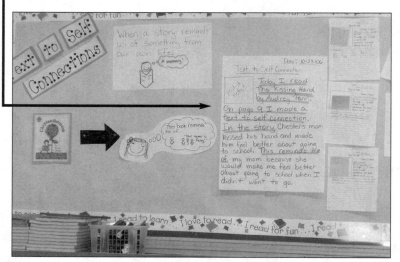

FIGURE 11.18

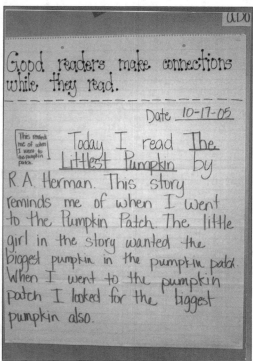

These teaching charts show children how to think about text-to-self connections. The teaching wall displays thinking graphically for children in simple, clear terms drawings.

FIGURE 11.19 Writing Sample: Text-to-Self Connection

Date 10-31-06

Text to Self Connection

This reminds me of when I you to Panit a lot it was fun I was happy Because I panit a lot

Today I read grandma moses BY ALEXANDRA WALLNER. on page 18 I made a text to self connection. In the story the old lady had a show in tell about her paniting she add detalis on you panit. She panits a lots she is a good paniter she show everyone her paniting the people says that she a good paniter and she is a good paniter she love to panit a lot. This reminds me of when I you to panit a lot it was fun I was happy Because I panit a lot.

Unit 4

Making Text-to-Text Connections

In this unit, students identify a part of a book that reminds them of another book (or text or a poem or a song). Again they jot the connection on a sticky note and attach it to the corresponding page in the book. The focus is on

- identifying types of texts and genres: poems, fiction, nonfiction, and so on
- connecting to characters from other books
- focusing on characters' feelings, thoughts, and actions and relating these to characters in other texts
- placing the sticky note on the page of the book where the connection was made
- referring back to the sticky note to jog thinking

Figure 11.20 is the map for this unit; Figure 11.21 shows some teaching charts from the unit; and Figures 11.22 and 11.23 are samples of student work produced during the unit. Response frames are available on pp. 184, 193, and 194.

FIGURE 11.20 Plan for "Making Text-to-Text Connections" Unit

Unit 4

Reading Workshop Four-Week Minilesson Map
Unit of Study: Making Text-to-Text Connections

Monday	Tuesday	Wednesday	Thursday	Friday
Introduce chart and model response text-to-text connections	Teach sticky notes procedure	Share student examples and teacher model for bulletin board	Focus on quality of sticky notes and share student examples	Discuss text-to-text connections How books can remind us of other books
Model how to expand thinking. Be specific when writing text-to-text response	Review how books can remind us of other books	Review model of current response sheet Prepare students for new response sheet	Extended writing format—introduce new poster, and new response sheet Focus on writing more	Focus on part 1 of response sheet "Today I read ____"
Share student examples of part 1	Focus on part 2 of response sheet, making it a small retelling of just that part "In the story . . ."	Share student examples of part 2	Focus on part 3 "This reminds me of . . ."	Share student examples of part 3
Model how to add details to connections	Model how to make the writing come alive in the reader's mind. Is your connection interesting?	Focus—how are we using our precious reading time?	Review parts 1–3 of response sheet with details	

Some days are intentionally left blank so they can be filled in as unit of study develops, based on students' needs.

FIGURE 11.21A

FIGURE 11.21B

Notice how the teaching wall (Figure 11.21A) scaffolds how to make a text-to-text connection, guiding the children to compare two texts. The teacher has defined a text-to-text connection in Figures 11.21A&B and gives an example in Figure 11.21C. These wall charts support Rosaura's thinking (Figure 11.22) and her ability to write a text-to-text connection independently during the workshop.

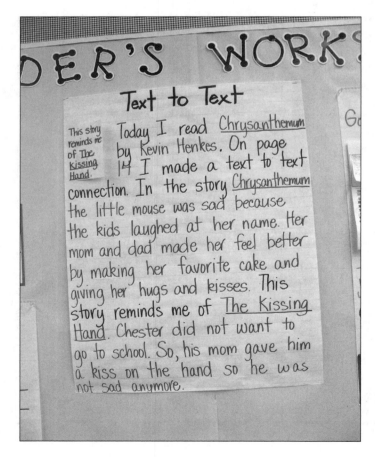

FIGURE 11.21C

Chapter Eleven

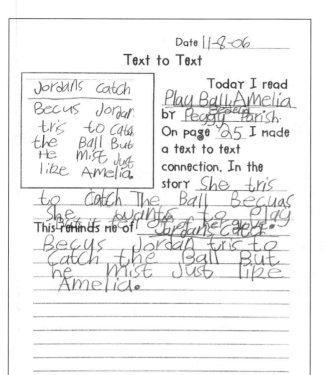

FIGURE 11.22 Writing Sample: Rosaura's Text-to-Text Connections

Date 11-8-06

Text to Text

Jordan's Catch

Becus Jordan tris to Catch the Ball But He Mist Just like Amelia.

Today I read Play Ball, Amelia by Peggy Parish. On page 25 I made a text to text connection. In the story She tris to Catch The Ball Becuas She wants to play She wants to play. This reminds me of Jordans Catch Becus Jordan tris to Catch the Ball But he Mist Just like Amelia.

Jenny's writing sample (Figure 11.23) shows how she was able to write a text-to-text connection without using the frame provided for Rosaura in Figure 11.22. Often teachers begin with the frame response sheet, and then move children to the response sheet with only lines. By doing so they release responsibility to the children for thinking through the connection and the writing.

FIGURE 11.23

Date 12/1/06

Text to Text

Chrys unthnmem

They both had no firend but at the end They both have firend.

Today I read Wemberly Worried by Kevin Henkes. On page 30 a text to text connection. In the story Wemberly went to school and saw Jewel but there one thing that people didn't know they both have in comit. This remind me of Chrysantmem because they both had no firend but at the end they but have firend.

Unit 5

Making Text-to-World Connections

In this unit, students identify a part of a book that reminds them of something in the world, either local or global: places and events they are aware of from newscasts, television shows, movies, and interactions with the adults in their lives. Again, children note the connection on a sticky note and attach it to the corresponding page in the book. The focus is on

- explaining what a world connection is
- relating information in texts to knowledge children have
- guiding children to connect their thinking to texts and prior knowledge
- guiding children to back up their thinking with evidence from the text and their knowledge
- helping children share information they know
- summarizing information
- adding details to text connections

Figure 11.24 is the map for this unit; Figures 11.25 through 11.29 show some teaching charts from the unit; and Figures 11.30 through 11.32 are samples of student work produced during the unit. Response frames are available on pp. 185, 193, and 194.

Hollie and Pam's Teaching Tips

- We work on text-to-world connections in January and February, after children have been introduced to and understand text-to-self connections, because text-to-world connections are harder for them to grasp.
- Many children's books deal with weather. In the San Joaquin valley, where we live, winter weather has a big impact on our community's agricultural economy. January often includes extreme weather conditions. We like to bring in the cover of our local newspaper after a rainstorm or overnight freeze to make text-to-world connections.
- We develop community understanding by focusing on Dr. Martin Luther King Jr.'s birthday and prompting our students to think about how people have impacted our community and our lives. We help them look for qualities in the characters in their books that remind them of things that are valuable in their community and qualities they respect in mentors and leaders they know.

FIGURE 11.24 Plan for "Making Text-to-World Connections" Unit

Reading Workshop Four-Week Minilesson Map
Unit of Study: Making Text-to-World Connections

Unit 5

Monday	Tuesday	Wednesday	Thursday	Friday
Introduce chart and model response—Movie or TV connection	Teach sticky notes procedure for making text-to-world connections	Share student examples and teacher model for teaching board	Introduce response sheet Focus on sticky notes and share student examples	Add to teaching chart, model response
Focus on sticky notes—procedure and quality—and share student examples	Share student responses—what does a good sticky note state?	Add to chart, model response—write about something we know	Review response sheet for week three	
Focus on part 1 of the response sheet—introduce new writing format "Today I read ____"	Share student examples of part 1	Focus on part 2, making it a small retelling of just that part "In the story . . ."	Share student examples of part 2	Focus on part 3 "This reminds me of . . ."
Share student examples of part 3	Model how to add details to our connections	Model how to make the connection come alive in your reader's mind	Review—how are we using our precious reading time?	Review parts 1–3 of response sheet with details

Some days are intentionally left blank so they can be filled in as unit of study develops, based on students' needs.

FIGURE 11.25

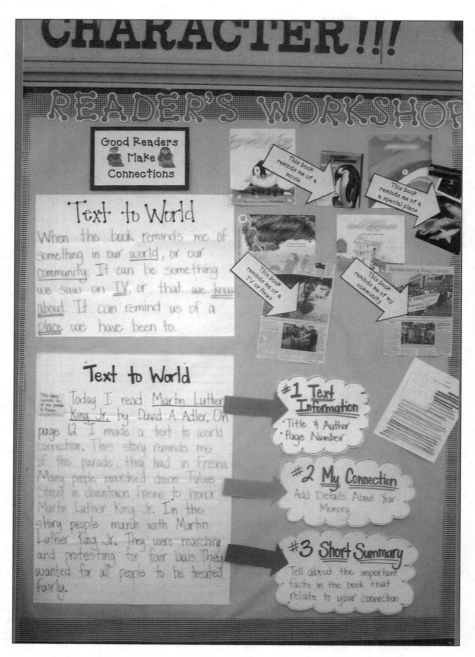

Text-to-world connections are trickier for young children to grasp if they don't have a lot of experiences thinking about text and thinking about world events, issues, places, and things. Figure 11.25 models what a text-to-world connection is, and then shows the children exactly how to begin writing the response. Of course, children are not marked down if their writing differs from the example. This is only a model to guide and support their thinking and independent writing about books.

FIGURE 11.26

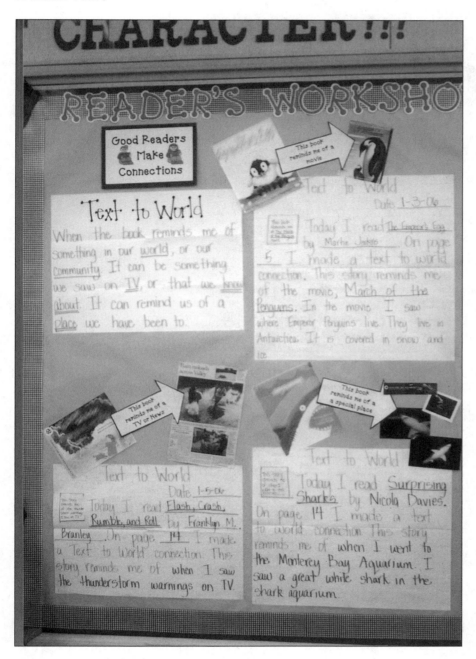

Figure 11.26 is another example of a teaching wall demonstrating text-to-world thinking. Each chart on the wall was used for two to three mini-lessons, and the material on the wall grew as the unit developed. Figures 11.27, 11.28, and 11.29 model connections that children *might* make between a book and movies, the news, or a special place.

FIGURE 11.27 Teacher Model: "Reminds Me of a Movie"

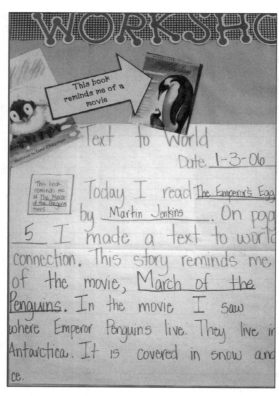

FIGURE 11.28 Teacher Model: "Reminds Me of TV or News"

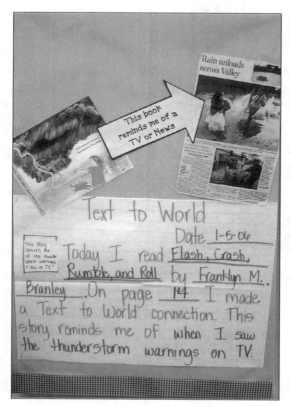

FIGURE 11.29 Teacher Model: "Reminds Me of a Special Place"

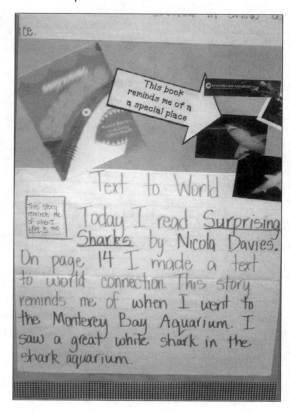

FIGURE 11.30 Writing Sample: Making Text-to-World Connections

Date January 17, 2006

Text to World

This reminds me of going to the beach.

Today I read
Ocean Life Tide Pool Creatures
By: Alice Leanhardt. On page 1
I made a text to world connection.
This story reminds me of going to
the beach because this tells me about
ocean creatures like a starfish, a sea
anemenone and other creatures on this
book. The ocean reminds me of the beach
but the ocean is a little different from the beach but on page 1 it shows
the water of the ocean. Theres not that much creatures on the beach but
it sometimes gets the creatures from the ocean. Anyways the beach has sand
but the ocean doesn't.

FIGURE 11.31 Writing Sample: Making Text-to-World Connections

Date 1-2.06

Text to World

This story reminds me of when we had a storm.

Today I read Huricanes have eyes but can't see. By Melvin Berger. On Page 9 I made a text to world connection. This story remineds me of when fresno had a storm. We had a 4.7 storm. Before the storm happend there was darn clouds. During the storm there was thunder. After the storm there was a blue sky and white clouds. In the story there was pictures that showed a thunder storm and lightning. It looked just like the thunder storm that we had. Then it shows a before picture and an after picture.

FIGURE 11.32 Writing Sample: Making Text-to-World Connections

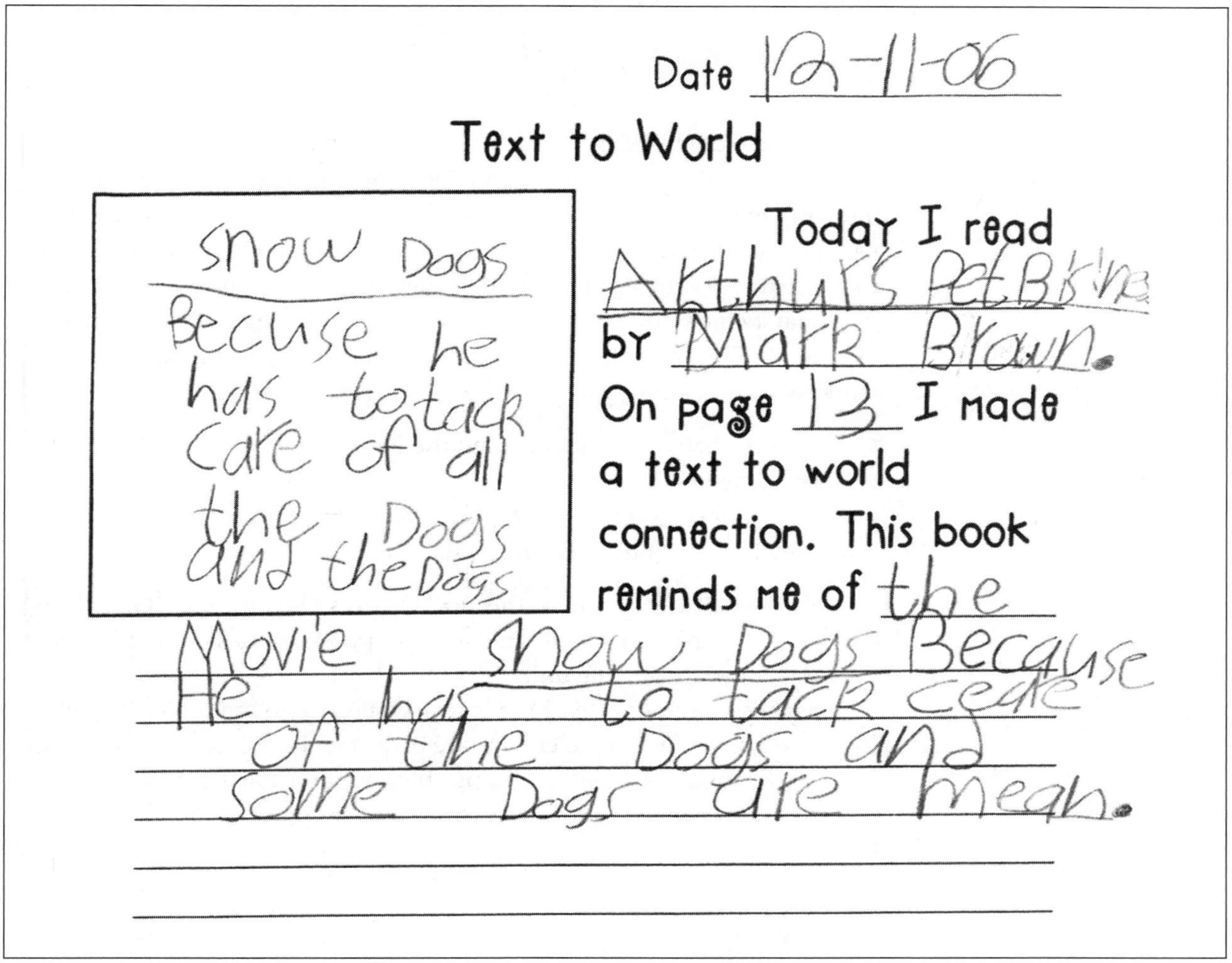

Date 12-11-06

Text to World

snow Dogs
Becuse he
has to tack
care of all
the Dogs
and the Dogs

Today I read
Arthurs pet Bisne
by Mark Brown.
On page 13 I made
a text to world
connection. This book
reminds me of the
Movie snow Dogs Because
He has to tack cede
of the Dogs and
some Dogs are mean.

Unit 6

Identifying Text Structure

In this unit, students identify story elements—characters, setting, plot, and resolution—in the context of how fiction is organized (beginning, middle, and end), the problem that arises, and how the problem is solved. Students also identify structural differences between fiction and nonfiction. (Nonfiction structural elements are main idea, details, conclusion, and print features that include but are not limited to labels, diagrams, table of contents, and index.) Children choose the type of response they write based on the genre they are reading. The focus is on

- differences between fiction and nonfiction
- story elements
- nonfiction text structures
- text features that help comprehension

Figure 11.33 is the map for this unit; Figures 11.34 through 11.36 show some teaching charts from the unit; and Figure 11.37 is a sample of student work produced during the unit.

Response frames for teaching text structure are found on pp. 203–06. Response frames for story elements are on p. 186. Response frames focused on character analysis are found on pp. 189, 195, and 196. Response frames that guide and help comprehension are found on pp. 189–91.

FIGURE 11.33 Plan for "Identifying Text Structure" Unit

Unit 6

Reading Workshop Four-Week Minilesson Map
Unit of Study: Identifying Text Structure

Monday	Tuesday	Wednesday	Thursday	Friday
Introduce chart and model response—beginning, middle, end. Use sheet A-24	Focus on genre. Model using a response sheet to wonder, find facts, or visualize.	Focus on sticky notes and share student examples. Model on appropriate response sheet.	Focus on characters and setting—teach how to identify them in text.	Model a response using story element response sheet
Introduce teaching chart and model response—main idea, details, conclusion	Review what a main idea is	Discuss—how do the details support the main idea?	Focus on conclusions—model writing a response focused on the end.	Share student work—who is identifying main idea, details, conclusion?
Introduce chart and model response—problem and solution	Discuss—the problem drives the plot!	Focus on solution—model writing a response identifying resolution	Share student work—who is focused on problem–solution?	
Introduce chart and model response—text features	Share student responses focused on text features	Show how to write detailed response: "From this book I learned . . ."		

Some days are intentionally left blank so they can be filled in as unit of study develops, based on students' needs.

FIGURE 11.34

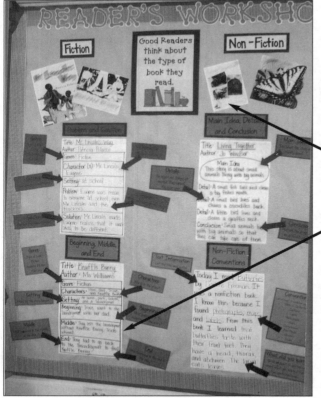

This teaching wall (Figure 11.34) developed section by section as the teacher presented information on text structure. On the left side of the board, she gives two examples of story structure. She uses the paper blocks to write descriptions of her thinking and places an arrow close by so children can refer to the chart for help independently. The right side shows children how to identify non-fiction text structure.

FIGURE 11.35

Figure 11.35 is a close-up of how the teacher analyzed the book *Mr. Lincoln's Way* by Patricia Polacco for story structure. The story elements she modeled are character, setting, problem and solution.

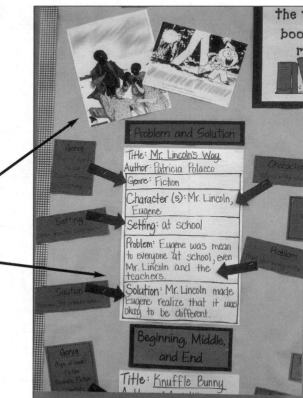

FIGURE 11.36

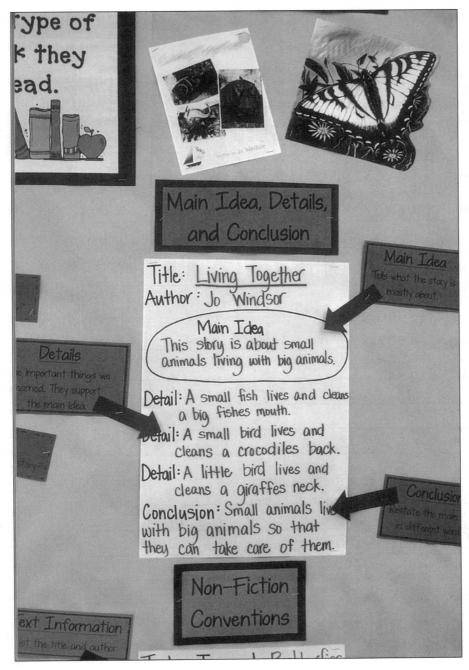

Figure 11.36 is a close-up of how the teacher analyzed the book *Living Together* by Jo Windsor for text structure. The nonfiction text elements she highlights include main idea, supporting details, and conclusion.

FIGURE 11.37 Writing Sample: Identifying Story Structure

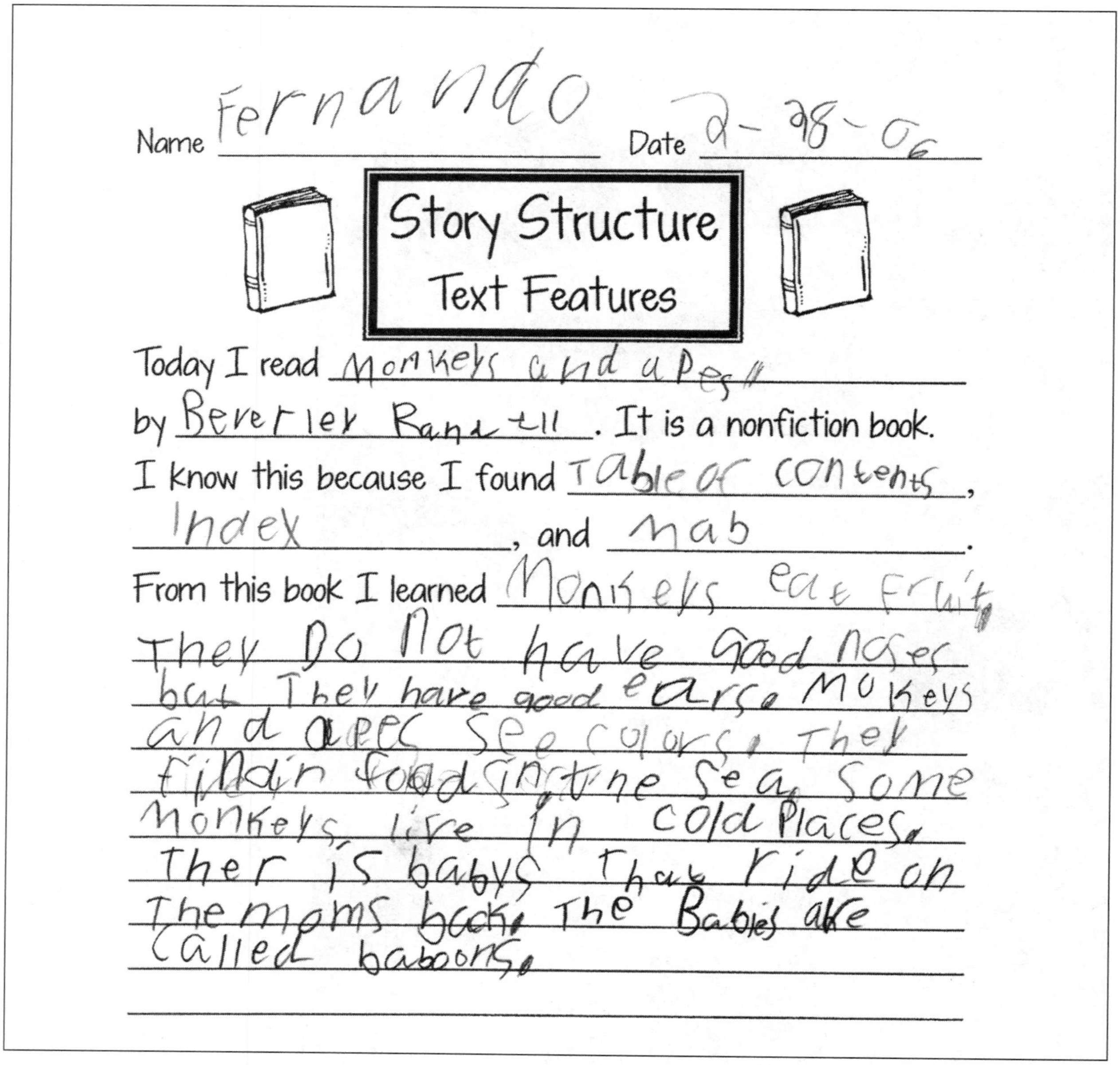

Name _Fernando_   Date _2-28-06_

Story Structure
Text Features

Today I read _Monkeys and apes"_
by _Beverley Randell_ . It is a nonfiction book.
I know this because I found _Table of contents_ ,
Index , and _map_ .
From this book I learned _Monkeys eat fruit_
They Do not have good noses
but They have good ears. Mokeys
and apes see colors. They
find food in the sea. some
monkeys live in cold places.
ther is babys that ride on
The moms back. The Babies are
called baboons.

Unit 7

Comparing and Contrasting
Text Structures

In this unit, students compare the structural features or story elements of two pieces of text. They learn to dig deeper and focus on their thinking in their comparisons. The focus is on

- comparing text features: including author, genre, characters, setting, main idea, nonfiction conventions, plot, and resolution (problem and solution)
- using two sticky notes: one to record similarities, one to record differences
- using a Venn diagram to compare and contrast texts
- thinking deeply about what the texts are saying
- using three response frames: Venn diagram, T-chart, and sticky-note recording sheet (see the appendix, pages 197–202)

Figure 11.38 is the map for this unit; Figures 11.39 through 11.41 show some teaching charts from the unit; Figures 11.42 and 11.43 are samples of student work produced during the unit.

Response frames focusing on compare and contrast are found on pp. 197–202.

FIGURE 11.38 Plan for "Comparing and Contrasting Text Structures" Unit

Reading Workshop Four-Week Minilesson Map
Unit of Study: Comparing and Contrasting Text Structures

Unit 7

	Monday	Tuesday	Wednesday	Thursday	Friday
	Introduce chart (How can we compare two books), model writing a response with narrative text	Model a response using narrative text	Share student examples from previous days' reading journals	Focus on sticky notes Ensure students use them correctly on the response sheet	Review chart, how we can compare two books Focus on comparing narrative and nonfiction
	Introduce new response format: T-chart	Share student examples—T-chart response paper	Model response again—T-chart	Model how to dig deeper with our thinking—what isn't on the cover of the book!	Share student work—who's digging deeper?
	Introduce new response format: Venn diagram	Model a response using Venn diagram	What makes our thinking deeper? Explore ways to help students contrast books	Share student work—who's digging deeper? Use a Venn diagram example	
	Review all three models of response sheets	Share student responses from any response sheet. Discuss why the examples are good thinking and comprehending.	Review—how are we using our precious reading time?		

Some days are intentionally left blank so they can be filled in as unit of study develops, based on students' needs.

Chapter Eleven

FIGURE 11.39

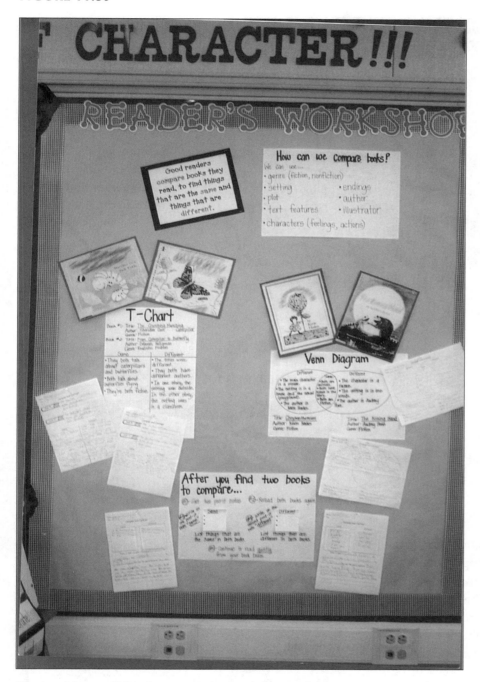

The teaching wall for the comparing and contrasting text structure unit teaches students various ways to think about texts. During various mini-lesson the teacher modeled a Venn diagram, a T-chart, and how to write a response using sticky notes to jot information. All three of these methods guide children to think about similarities and differences between texts. All three of these models for thinking help children be successful when synthesizing new information into a written response.

FIGURE 11.40

Figure 11.40 is a close-up of how the teacher scaffolded student thinking using sticky notes. She carefully wrote the steps out on the chart so that the children could visualize themselves moving through the exercise, eventually owning the strategy of text comparisons for themselves.

FIGURE 11.41

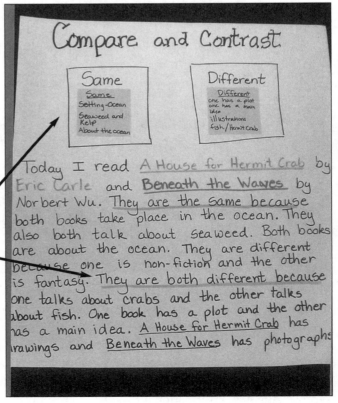

Figure 11.41 is a teacher-written sample modeling the same–different comparison. Notice in Figures 11.42 and 11.43 how the teacher's modeling made it easy for the children to write a response independently. In Figure 11.42 Justine created a bulleted list and in Figure 11.43 Brisa wrote her jots on the sticky notes and then wrote out a response using the frame. Brisa is an English learner, so the frame gave her thinking a jump start.

FIGURE 11.42 Writing Sample: Comparing and Contrasting Text Structures

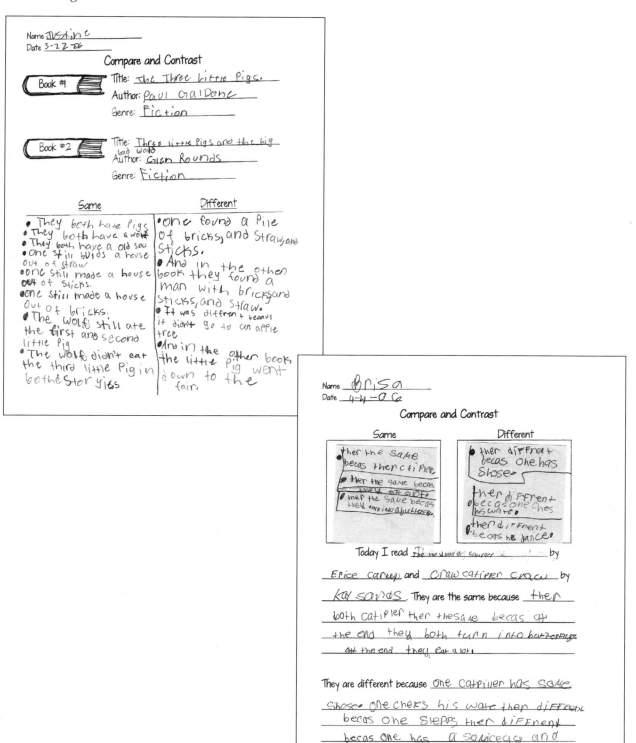

Name Justin C
Date 3-22-06

Compare and Contrast

Book #1

Title: The Three Little Pigs.
Author: Paul Galdone
Genre: Fiction

Book #2

Title: Three little Pigs and the big bad wolf
Author: Glen Rounds
Genre: Fiction

Same	Different
• They both have Pigs • They both have a wolf • They both have a old saw • One still buids a house out of straw • one still made a house out of sticks. • one still made a house out of bricks. • The wolf still ate the first and second little Pig • The wolf didn't eat the third little Pig in bothe Stor yies	• one found a Pile of bricks, and straw, and sticks. • And in the other book they found a man with bricks and sticks, and straw. • It was different becaus it didn't go to an apple tree • And in the other book the little pig went down to the fair.

Name Brisa
Date 4-4-06

Compare and Contrast

Same	Different
• ther the same becas ther c fi Peer • ther the same becas theu bot eeloff • ther the same becas they turn into a butterfly	• ther diffrent becas one has shose. • ther diffrent becas one ches his wate • ther diffrent becas he pance

Today I read The _____ caterper _____ by

Erice careey and craw catiper craew by

Kay sandes. They are the same because ther

both catiPler ther thesame becas at

the end they both turn into buttereys

at the end they eat a lot

They are different because one catPiller has same

shose. one cheks his wate then diffrent

becas one steppe then diffrent

becas one has a somiceye and

they do not have same of the

Fod but he gowse to the shop.

FIGURE 11.43 Writing Sample: Comparing and Contrasting Text Structures

Appendix

A-1

This belongs to _____   This belongs to _____

Sight Words		Sight Words	
1		1	
2		2	
3		3	
4		4	
5		5	
6		6	
7		7	
8		8	
9		9	
10		10	

A–2

Books! Books!

Name _____ Date _____

Appendixes

Favorite Part

Name _____ Date _____

This is my favorite part of the book: _____

A–4

Retelling

Name _____ Date _____

Book Title _____

Beginning	My Picture
Middle	
End	

A-5   Books! Books!

Name _____ Date _____

Book Title _____

┌──┐
│   │
│   │
│   │
│   │
│   │
│   │
│   │
│   │
│   │
└──┘

_____

_____

_____

_____

_____

Favorite Part

Name _____ Date _____

Book Title _____

On page _____ is my favorite part of the book I read. This is why:

_____

_____

_____

_____

Text-to-Self Connection

Name _____ Date _____

```
┌─────────────────────────────────────────────────────────────────┐
│                                                                   │
│                                                                   │
│                                                                   │
│                                                                   │
│                                                                   │
│                                                                   │
│                                                                   │
│                                                                   │
│                                                                   │
│                                                                   │
│                                                                   │
└─────────────────────────────────────────────────────────────────┘
```

On page _____ I made a text-to-self connection. This is what the book reminded me of:

_____

_____

_____

_____

Text-to-Text Connection

Name _____ Date _____

[ ]

On page _____ I made a text-to-text connection. The book _____
_____ reminded me of another book I read.
This is what I thought about:

_____

_____

_____

_____

Text-to-World Connection

Name _____ Date _____

[blank drawing box]

On page _____ I made a text-to-world connection. The book
_____ reminded me of something
I know about, have seen, or have heard. This is what I thought about:

_____

_____

_____

_____

© 2008 by Nancy Akhavan from *The Title I Teacher's Guide to Teaching Reading, K–3*. Portsmouth, NH: Heinemann.

Story Elements

Name _____ Date _____

Book Title _____

Setting	
	_____
	_____
Character	_____
	_____
	_____
	_____
Events	_____
	_____
	_____
Resolution	_____
	_____
	_____

A-11   Characters

Name _____ Date _____

Picture of my character	I read the book _____.
	Let me tell you about a character in the book.
	_____
	_____
	_____

_____

_____

_____

_____

_____

A-12   Retelling

Name _____ Date _____

Today I read the book _____.
This is what happened in the book.

First

Next

Then

Last

Appendixes

A–13   Wondering

Name _____ Date _____

┌─────────────────┐   I read the book
│   │   _____.
│   ?   │
│   │   I had questions while I was reading.
│   │   I wondered . . .
└─────────────────┘

_____

_____

_____

_____

_____

_____

_____

© 2008 by Nancy Akhavan from *The Title I Teacher's Guide to Teaching Reading, K–3*. Portsmouth, NH: Heinemann.

Appendixes   **189**

A-14　　　　　　Nonfiction Fact Finding

Name _____ Date _____

List 2-3 facts you learned here, then write about them below.

Today I read: _____
I learned . . .

_____

_____

_____

_____

A-15   Visualization

Name _____ Date _____

Book Title _____

+---+
| |
| |
| |
| |
| |
| |
| |
| |
| |
| |
| |
| |
| |
+---+

While I was reading, I was making mental pictures. I could see . . .

_____

_____

_____

_____

A-16  Retelling

Name _____ Date _____

Place your sticky note here.

_____
_____
_____
_____
_____
_____
_____

_____

_____

_____

Appendixes

A-17   Text-to- _____ Connection

Name _____ Date _____

Today I read

_____

by _____. On

page _____ I made a text-to-

_____ connection. In the

story _____

_____

_____

Put your sticky note here.

This reminds me of _____

_____

_____

_____

_____

Fill in the blank at the top of the page stating if you made a text-to-self,
text-to-text, or text-to-world connection.

A-18   Text-to-_____ Connection

Name _____ Date _____

+-----------------------------+   _____
| |
| | _____
| |
| | _____
| |
| | _____
| |
| | _____
| Put your sticky note here. |
+-----------------------------+   _____

_____

_____

_____

_____

Fill in the blank at the top of the page stating if you made a text-to-self, text-to-text, or text-to-world connection.

A-19   Character Study

Name: _____

Date: _____

Title: _____

Author:_____

Genre: _____

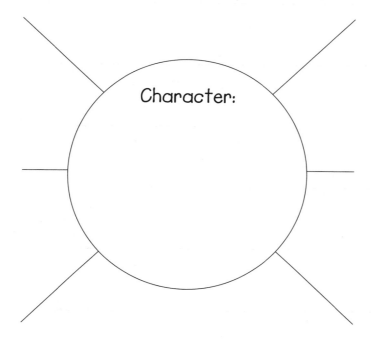

Character:

_____

_____

_____

_____

Character Study (page 2)

Compare and Contrast

Name: _____

Date: _____

Book #1

Title: _____

Author: _____

Genre: _____

Book #2

Title: _____

Author: _____

Genre: _____

Same	Different

Same (continued)	Different (continued)

Compare and Contrast

Name _____ Date _____

┌─────────────────────────────┐
│   │ Today I read
│   │
│   │ _____
│   │
│   │ by _____
│   │
│   │ and _____
│   │
│   │ by _____ .
│   │
│   │ These two books are the same
│ Put your sticky note here. │
│   │ because _____
└─────────────────────────────┘

_____

_____

These two books are different because _____

_____

_____

_____

_____

Compare and Contrast

Name _____ Date _____

Put your sticky note here.	Put your sticky note here.

Today I read _____ by

_____ and _____ by

_____. They are the same because _____

_____

_____

_____

_____

They are different because _____

_____

_____

_____

_____

Compare and Contrast

Name: _____ Date: _____

Different

Same

Different

Title: _____
Author: _____
Genre: _____

Title: _____
Author: _____
Genre: _____

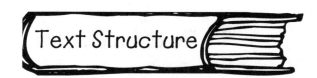

Name: _____ Date: _____

Title: _____

Author: _____

Genre:
Characters:
Setting:
Beginning:
Middle:
End:

A-25   Text Structure

Name: _____ Date: _____

Title: _____

Author: _____

Main Idea:

Detail:

_____

_____

_____

Detail:

_____

_____

_____

Detail:

_____

_____

_____

Conclusion:

_____

_____

_____

A-26

Text Structure
Print Features

Name _____ Date _____

Today I read _____

by _____. It is a nonfiction book.

I know this because I found _____,

_____, and _____.

From this book I learned _____

_____

_____

_____

_____

_____

Appendixes

A-27  Favorite Part

Name _____ Date _____

┌──┐
│   │
│   │
│   │
│   │
│   │
│   │
│   │
└──┘

_____

_____

_____

_____

_____

Name _____ Date _____

_____

_____

_____

_____

_____

_____

_____

_____

Use this additional page with any response frame.

Children's Literature References

Almada, Patricia. 2004. *Chico*. Barrington, IL: Rigby.

Asch, Frank. 1999. *Moonbear's Skyfire*. New York: Simon and Schuster.

Banks, Kate. 2002. *Close Your Eyes*. New York: Farrar, Straus and Giroux.

Beach, Judi K. 2003. *Names for Snow*. New York: Hyperion Books for Children.

Blume, Judy. 1985. *The Pain and the Great One*. New York: Bantam Double-day Dell.

Bonning, Tony. 2004. *Snog the Frog*. Hauppauge, NY: Barron's.

Bryson, Theresa. 2003. *Farm Alarm*. Pelham, NY: Benchmark Education.

Cannon, Janell. 2004. *Pinduli*. San Diego: Harcourt.

Cowley, Joy. 1986. *I Can Jump*. Bothell, WA: Wright Group.

———. 2001. *The Kick-a-Lot Shoes*. Bothell, WA: Wright Group.

Creech, Sharon. 2000. *Fishing in the Air*. New York: Joanna Cotler.

Crimi, Carolyn. 2000. *Don't Need Friends*. New York: Scholastic.

Dealey, Erin. 2002. *Goldie Locks Has Chicken Pox*. New York: Scholastic.

DiPucchio, Kelly. 2005. *What's the Magic Word?* New York: HarperCollins.

Edwards, Pamela Duncan. 2003. *Rosie's Roses*. New York: HarperCollins.

Elliot, Laura Malone. 2002. *Hunter's Best Friend at School*. New York: HarperCollins.

Falconer, Ian. 2000. *Olivia*. New York: Atheneum.

Fletcher, Ralph. 2003. *Hello, Harvest Moon*. New York: Clarion.

Geeslin, Campbell. 2004. *Elena's Serenade*. New York: Atheneum Books for Young Readers.

George, Kristine O'Connell. 2002. *Little Dog and Duncan*. New York: Clarion.

Giles, Jenny. 1997. *Sally and the Sparrows*. Barrington, IL: Rigby.

Henkes, Kevin. 1993a. *Ouch*. New York: Greenwillow.

———. 1993b. *Owen*. New York: Greenwillow.

———. 1995. *Julius, the Baby of the World*. New York: Harper Trophy.

———. 1996a. *Chrysanthemum*. New York: Harper Trophy.

———. 1996b. *Lily's Purple Plastic Purse*. New York: Greenwillow.

Hindley, Judy. 2002. *Rosy's Visitors*. Cambridge, MA: Candlewick.

Hoban, Russell. 1976. *A Baby Sister for Frances*. New York: Harper Trophy.

Hobbie, Holly. 2003a. *Toot and Puddle: Charming Opal*. New York: Little, Brown.

———. 2003b. *Toot and Puddle: The New Friend*. New York: Little, Brown.

Iverson, Sandra. 2000. *Mr. Bumblesticker Goes to the Zoo*. DeSoto, TX: Wright Group.

Kline, Suzy. 1998. *Horrible Harry and the Green Slime*. New York: Puffin.

Lawler, Janet. 2003. *If Kisses Were Colors*. New York: Dial.

Lionni, Leo. 1969. *Alexander and the Wind-Up Mouse*. New York: Alfred A. Knopf.

McHenry, E. B. 2004. *Poodlena*. New York: Bloomsbury.

Parish, Peggy. 1992. *Amelia Bedelia*. I Can Read, Book 2. New York: Harper Trophy.

Perkins, Lynne Rae. 2003. *Snow Music*. New York: Greenwillow.

Randell, Beverley. 1996. *Baby Bear's Present*. Barrington, IL: Rigby.

———. 2004a. *Lizard Loses His Tail*. Barrington, IL: Rigby.

———. 2004b. *Ten Little Garden Snails*. Barrington, IL: Rigby.

Ryder, Joanne. 2004. *Won't You Be My Kissaroo?* San Diego: Gulliver.

Rylant, Cynthia. 1998. *Scarecrow*. San Diego: Voyager.

———. 2002. *The Ticky Tacky Doll*. San Diego: Harcourt.

———. 2005. *The Stars Will Shine*. New York: HarperCollins.

Schertle, Alice. 2003. *When the Moon Is High*. New York: HarperCollins.

Schlein, Miraim. 2004. *Little Raccoon's Big Question*. New York: Greenwillow.

Simmons, Jane. 1997. *Come Along Daisy*. New York: Scholastic.

Smith, Alastair, and Laura Howell. 2004. *On the Beach*. London: Usborne.

Soto, Gary. 1996. *The Old Man and His Door*. New York: Putnam and Grosset.

Tafuri, Nancy. 1998. *I Love You, Little One*. New York: Scholastic.

Vail, Rachel. 2005. *Sometimes I'm Bombaloo*. New York: Scholastic.

Wells, Rosemary. 1997. *Bunny Cakes*. New York: Puffin.

———. 2000. *Max Cleans Up*. New York: Puffin.

Wilson, Karma. 2003. *Bear Wants More*. New York: Simon and Schuster.

References

Adams, Marilyn Jager. 1990. *Beginning to Read: Thinking and Learning About Print*. Cambridge, MA: MIT Press.

Afflerbach, Peter. 2002. "Teaching Reading Self-Assessment Strategies." In *Comprehension Instruction: Research-Based Best Practices*, ed. Cathy Collins Block and Michael Pressley, 96–114. New York: Guilford.

Akhavan, Nancy. 2004. *How to Align Literacy Instruction, Assessment and Standards and Achieve Results You Never Dreamed Possible*. Portsmouth, NH: Heinemann.

———. 2006. *Help! My Kids Don't All Speak English: How to Set Up a Language Workshop in Your Linguistically Diverse Classroom*. Portsmouth, NH: Heinemann.

Allington, Richard L. 2001. *What Really Matters for Struggling Readers: Designing Research-Based Programs*. New York: Addison Wesley.

Allington, Richard L., and Patricia M. Cunningham. 1999. *Classrooms That Work*. 2d ed. New York: Longman.

———. 2001. *Schools That Work: Where All Children Read and Write*. 2d ed. New York: Allyn and Bacon.

American Educational Research Association (AERA). 2004a. "Closing the Gap: High Achievement for Students of Color." *Research Points: Essential Information for Education Policy* 2(3): 1–4.

———. 2004b. "English Language Learners: Boosting Academic Achievement." *Research Points: Essential Information for Education Policy* 2(1): 1–4.

Au, Kathryn H., Betsy M. Baker, Patricia A. Edwards, James V. Hoffman, Adria F. Klein, Diane L. Larsen, John W. Logan, Lesley Mandel Morrow, and Timothy Shanahan. 1999. *Using Multiple Methods of Beginning Reading Instruction*. A Position Statement of the International Reading Association. Newark, DE: International Reading Association.

Baker, Linda. 2002. "Metacognition in Comprehension Instruction." In *Comprehension Instruction: Research-Based Best Practices*, ed. Cathy Collins Block and Michael Pressley, 77–95. New York: Guilford.

Baker, Tanya N., Julie Dube Hackett, and Jeffrey D. Wilhelm. 2001. *Strategic Reading: Guiding Students to Lifelong Literacy, 6–12*. Portsmouth, NH: Heinemann.

Barton, Paul E. 2004. "Why Does the Gap Persist?" *Educational Leadership* 62(3): 9–13.

Bear, Donald R., Marcia Invernizzi, Shane R. Templeton, and Francine Johnston. 1996. *Words Their Way: Word Study for Phonics, Vocabulary, and Spelling*. 3d ed. Upper Saddle River, NJ: Prentice Hall.

Beaver, Joetta. 2004. *Developmental Reading Assessment*. Parsippany, NJ: Pearson Education.

Block, Cathy Collins, and Susan E. Israel. 2004. "The ABCs of Performing Highly Effective Think Alouds." *The Reading Teacher* 58(2): 154–67.

Block, Cathy Collins, and Michael Pressley, eds. 2002. *Comprehension Instruction: Research-Based Best Practices*. New York: Guilford.

———. 2003. "Best Practices in Comprehension Instruction." In *Best Practices in Literacy Instruction*, 2d ed., ed. Lesley Mandel Morrow, Linda B. Gambrell, and Michael Pressley, 111–26. New York: Guilford.

California State Department of Education. English Language Arts Standards, Grade Three. Retrieved August 22, 2007, from http://www.cde.ca.gov/be/st/ss/enggrade3.asp.

Calkins, Lucy. 1994. *The Art of Teaching Writing*. Portsmouth, NH: Heinemann.

———. 2001. *The Art of Teaching Reading*. New York: Addison Wesley.

Calkins, Lucy, and Shelley Harwayne. 1987. *The Writing Workshop: A World of Difference*. Portsmouth, NH: Heinemann.

Cambourne, Brian. 2002. "Holistic, Integrated Approaches to Reading and Language Arts Instruction: The Constructivist Framework of an Instructional Theory." In *What Research Has to Say About Reading Instruction*, ed. Alan E. Farstrup and S. Jay Samuels, 25–47. Newark, DE: International Reading Association.

Clay, Marie M. 2001. *Change Over Time in Children's Literacy Development*. Portsmouth, NH: Heinemann.

Cole, Ardith Davis. 2004. *When Reading Begins: The Teacher's Role in Decoding, Comprehension, and Fluency*. Portsmouth, NH: Heinemann.

Colt, Jackalyn, and Rebecca Mills. 2002. "Rocky Mountain Elementary School, Longmont, Colorado." In *Teaching Reading: Effective Schools, Accomplished Teachers*, ed. Barbara M. Taylor and P. David Pearson, 163–78. Mahwah, NJ: Lawrence Erlbaum.

Cummins, Jim. 1989. *Empowering Minority Students*. Sacramento: California Association for Bilingual Education.

———. 1991. *Empowering Culturally and Linguistically Diverse Students with Learning Problems*. ERIC EC Digest #E500. Arlington, VA: ERIC Clearinghouse on Disabilities and Gifted Education.

———. 2003. "Reading and the Bilingual Student: Fact and Friction." In *English Learners: Reaching the Highest Level of English Literacy*, ed. Gilbert G. Garcia, 2–33. Newark, DE: International Reading Association.

Cunningham, Patricia M., and James W. Cunningham. 2002. "What We Know About How to Teach Phonics." In *What Research Has to Say About Reading Instruction*, ed. Alan E. Farstrup and S. Jay Samuels, 87–109. Newark, DE: International Reading Association.

Darling-Hammond, Linda. 1997. *The Right to Learn: A Blueprint for Creating Schools That Work*. San Francisco: Jossey-Bass.

Diehl, Holly L. 2005. "Snapshots of Our Journey to Thoughtful Literacy." *The Reading Teacher* 59(1): 56–69.

Duffy, Gerald G. 2002. "The Case for Direct Explanation of Strategies." In *Comprehension Instruction: Researched-Based Best Practices*, ed. Cathy Collins Block and Michael Pressley, 28–41. New York: Guilford.

Durkin, Dolores. 1978–79. "What Classroom Observations Reveal About Reading Comprehension Instruction." *Reading Research Quarterly* 4: 481–533.

Farstrup, Alan E., and S. Jay Samuels, eds. 2002. "Note from the Editors." In *What Research Has to Say About Reading Instruction*, 3d ed., v–vi. Newark, DE: International Reading Association.

Fountas, Irene C., and Gay Su Pinnell. 1996. *Guided Reading: Good First Teaching for All Children*. Portsmouth, NH: Heinemann.

———. 1998. *Word Matters: Teaching Phonics and Spelling in the Reading/ Writing Classroom*. Portsmouth, NH: Heinemann.

———. 2000. *Guiding Readers and Writers: Teaching Comprehension, Genre and Content Literacy*. Portsmouth, NH: Heinemann.

———. 2004. *Word Study Lessons: Phonics, Spelling and Vocabulary*. Portsmouth, NH: Firsthand.

———. 2005. *The Fountas and Pinnell Leveled Book List, K–8*. 2006 ed. Portsmouth, NH: Heinemann.

———. 2006. *Teaching for Comprehending and Fluency: Thinking, Talking, and Writing About Reading, K–8*. Portsmouth, NH: Heinemann.

Galda, Lee, Gwynne Ellen Ash, and Bernice E. Cullinan. 2000. "Children's Literature." In *Handbook of Reading Research*, vol. 3, ed. Michael L. Kamil, Peter B. Mosenthal, P. David Pearson, and Rebecca Barr, 361–80. Mahwah, NJ: Lawrence Erlbaum.

Gavelek, James R., Taffy E. Raphael, Sandra M. Biondo, and Danhua Wang. 2000. "Integrated Literacy Instruction." In *Handbook of Reading Research*, vol. 3, ed. Michael L. Kamil, Peter B. Mosenthal, P. David Pearson, and Rebecca Barr, 587–608. Mahwah, NJ: Lawrence Erlbaum.

Gibbons, Pauline. 1991. *Learning to Learn in a Second Language*. Portsmouth, NH: Heinemann.

———. 2002. *Scaffolding Language, Scaffolding Learning: Teaching Second Language Learners in the Mainstream Classroom*. Portsmouth, NH: Heinemann.

Graves, Donald. 2003. *Writing: Teachers and Children at Work*. 20th anniv. ed. Portsmouth, NH: Heinemann.

Hale, Janice E. 2004. "How Schools Shortchange African American Children." *Educational Leadership* 62(3): 34–38.

Haycock, Kati. 2001. "Closing the Achievement Gap." *Educational Leadership* 58(6): 6–11.

———. 2001. "New Frontiers for a New Century." *Thinking K–16* 5(2): 1–2.

Henze, Rosemary, and Gilberto Arriaza. 2006. "Language and Reforming Schools: A Case of a Critical Approach to Language in Educational Leadership." *International Journal of Leadership in Education* 9(2): 157–77.

Hiebert, Elfrieda H., and Barbara M. Taylor. 2000. "Beginning Reading Instruction: Research on Early Interventions." In *Handbook of Reading Research*, vol. 3, ed. Michael L. Kamil, Peter B. Mosenthal, P. David Pearson, and Rebecca Barr, 455–82. Mahwah, NJ: Lawrence Erlbaum.

International Reading Association. 2000. "Providing Books and Other Print Materials for Classroom and School Libraries." A position statement of the International Reading Association. Newark, DE: International Reading Association.

Johnson, Joseph Jr. 2002. "High-Performing, High-Poverty, Urban Elementary Schools." In *Teaching Reading: Effective Schools, Accomplished Teachers*, ed. Barbara M. Taylor and P. David Pearson, 89–114. Mahwah, NJ: Lawrence Erlbaum.

Ketch, Ann. 2005. "Conversation: The Comprehension Connection." *The Reading Teacher* 59(1): 8–13.

Klenk, Laura, and Michael W. Kibby. 2000. "Re-Mediating Reading Difficulties: Appraising the Past, Reconciling the Present, Constructing the Future." In *Handbook of Reading Research*, vol. 3, ed. Michael L. Kamil, Peter B. Mosenthal, P. David Pearson, and Rebecca Barr, 667–90. Mahwah, NJ: Lawrence Erlbaum.

Krashen, Steven D. 1997. "Bridging Inequity with Books." *Educational Leadership* 55(4): 19–22.

———. 2003. *Explorations in Language Acquisition and Use*. Portsmouth, NH: Heinemann.

Liang, Lauren Aimonette, and Janice A. Dole. 2006. "Help with Teaching Reading Comprehension: Comprehension Instructional Frameworks." *The Reading Teacher* 59(8): 742–53.

Marzano, Robert. 2003. *What Works in Schools: Translating Research into Action*. Alexandria, VA: Association for Supervision and Curriculum Development.

Marzano, Robert J., Debra Pickering, and Jane E. Pollack. 2001. *Classroom Instruction That Works: Researched-Based Strategies for Increasing Student Achievement*. Alexandria, VA: Association for Supervision and Curriculum Development.

Mazzoni, Susan Anders, and Linda B. Gambrell. 2003. "Principles of Best Practice: Finding the Common Ground." In *Best Practices in Literacy Instruction*, ed. Lesley Mandel Morrow, Linda B. Gambrell, and Michael Pressley, 9–22. New York: Guilford.

McGee, Lea M., and Donald J. Richgels. 2003. *Designing Early Literacy Programs: Strategies for At-Risk Preschool and Kindergarten Children*. New York: Guilford.

McGill-Franzen, Anne, Courtney Zmack, Katie Solic, and Jacqueline Love Zeig. 2006. "The Confluence of Two Policy Mandates: Core Reading Programs and Third-Grade Retention in Florida." *The Elementary School Journal* 107: 67–91.

Mesmer, Heidi Anne E., and Priscilla L. Griffith. 2006. "Everybody's Selling It—But Just What Is Explicit, Systematic Phonics Instruction?" *The Reading Teacher* 59(4): 366–76.

Morris, Darrell, Janet W. Bloodgood, Richard G. Lomax, and Jan Perney. 2003. "Developmental Steps in Learning to Read: A Longitudinal Study in Kindergarten and First Grade." *Reading Research Quarterly* 38(3): 302–28.

Nagy, William E. 1988. *Teaching Vocabulary to Improve Reading Comprehension*. Newark, DE: International Reading Association.

Nagy, William E., and Richard C. Anderson. 1984. "How Many Words Are There in Printed School English?" *Reading Research Quarterly* 19: 304–30.

Nagy, William E., and Judith A. Scott. 2000. "Vocabulary Processes." In *Handbook of Reading Research*, vol. III, ed. Michael L. Kamil, Peter B. Mosenthal, P. David Pearson, and Rebecca Barr, 269–83. Mahwah, NJ: Lawrence Erlbaum.

National Center on Education and the Economy, New Standards Speaking and Listening Committee. 2001. *Speaking and Listening for Preschool Through Third Grade*. Pittsburgh: National Center on Education and the Economy.

National Institute of Child Health and Human Development (NICHD). 2000. *Report of the National Reading Panel. Teaching Children to Read: An Evidence-Based Assessment of the Scientific Research Literature on Reading and Its Implications for Reading Instruction*. NIH Publication No. 00-4769. Washington, DC: U.S. Government Printing Office.

Opitz, Michael F., and Michael P. Ford. 2001. *Reaching Readers: Flexible and Innovative Strategies for Guided Reading*. Portsmouth, NH: Heinemann.

Owocki, Gretchen. 2003. *Comprehension*. Portsmouth, NH: Heinemann.

Owocki, Gretchen, and Yetta Goodman. 2002. *Kidwatching: Documenting Children's Literacy Development*. Portsmouth, NH: Heinemann.

Pardo, Laura S. 2004. "What Every Teacher Needs to Know About Comprehension." *The Reading Teacher* 58(3): 272–80.

Patterson, Wendy A., Julie Jacobs Henry, Karen O'Quin, Maria A. Ceprano, and Elfreda A. Blue. 2003. "Investigating the Effectiveness of an Integrated Learning System on Early Emergent Readers." *Reading Research Quarterly* 38(2): 172–207.

Pearson, P. David, and Nell K. Duke. 2002. "Comprehension Instruction in the Primary Grades." In *Comprehension Instruction: Researched-Based Best Practices*, ed. Cathy Collins Block and Michael Pressley, 247–58. New York: Guilford.

Pearson, P. David, and Taffy E. Raphael. 2003. "Toward a More Complex View of Balance in the Literacy Curriculum." In *Best Practices in Literacy Instruction*, ed. Lesley Mandel Morrow, Linda B. Gambrell, and Michael Pressley, 23–42. New York: Guilford.

Pfeffer, Jeffrey, and Robert I. Sutton. 2000. *The Knowing-Doing Gap: How Smart Companies Turn Knowledge into Action*. Boston: Harvard Business School Press.

Pinnell, Gay Su, and Irene C. Fountas. 2003. *Phonics Lessons: Letters, Words, and How They Work, Grade 1*. Portsmouth, NH: Firsthand.

———. 2003. *Phonics Lessons: Letters, Words, and How They Work, Grade 2*. Portsmouth, NH: Firsthand.

Pressley, Michael. 2000. "What Should Comprehension Instruction Be the Instruction Of?" In *Handbook of Reading Research*, vol. III, ed. Michael L. Kamil, Peter B. Mosenthal, P. David Pearson, and Rebecca Barr, 545–62. Mahwah, NJ: Lawrence Erlbaum.

———. 2002a. "Metacognition and Self-Regulated Comprehension." In *What Research Has to Say About Reading Instruction*, ed. Alan E. Farstrup and S. Jay Samuels, 291–309. Newark, DE: International Reading Association.

———. 2002b. *Reading Instruction That Works: The Case for Balanced Teaching*. 2d ed. New York: Guilford.

Pressley, Michael, and Cathy Collins Block. 2002. "Summing Up: What Comprehension Instruction Could Be." In *Comprehension Instruction: Researched-Based Best Practices*, ed. Cathy Collins Block and Michael Pressley, 383–92. New York: Guilford.

Pressley, Michael, and Karen R. Harris. 2006. "Cognitive Strategies Instruction: From Basic Research to Classroom Instruction." In *Handbook of Educational Psychology*, 2d ed., ed. Patricia A. Alexander and Philip H. Winne, 265–86. Mahwah, NJ: Lawrence Erlbaum.

Pressley, Michael, Ruth Wharton-McDonald, Lisa M. Raphael, Kristen Bogner, and Alysia Roehrig. 2002. "Exemplary First Grade Teaching." In *Teaching Reading: Effective Schools, Accomplished Teachers*, ed. Barbara M. Taylor and P. David Pearson, 73–88. Mahwah, NJ: Lawrence Erlbaum.

Reeves, Douglas B. 2006. *The Learning Leader: How to Focus School Improvement for Better Results*. Alexandria, VA: Association for Supervision and Curriculum Development.

Richgels, Donald J. 2004. "Paying Attention to Language." *Reading Research Quarterly* 39(4): 470–77.

Samuels, S. Jay. 2002. "Reading Fluency: Its Development and Assessment." In *What Research Has to Say About Reading Instruction*, ed. Alan E. Farstrup and S. Jay Samuels, 166–83. Newark, DE: International Reading Association.

Samuels, S. Jay, D. LaBerge, and C. Bremer. 1978. "Units of Word Recognition: Evidence for Developmental Changes." *Journal of Verbal Learning and Verbal Behavior* 17: 715–20.

Saunders-Smith, Gail. 2002. *The Ultimate Guided Reading How-to Book: Building Literacy Through Small-Group Instruction*. Chicago, IL: Zephyr Press.

Scarcella, Robin. 2003. *Academic English: A Conceptual Framework*. Technical Report 2003-1. Irvine, CA: University of California Linguistic Minority Research Institute.

Schmoker, Mike. 2006. *Results Now: How We Can Achieve Unprecedented Improvements in Teaching and Learning*. Alexandria, VA: Association of Supervision and Curriculum Development.

Sinatra, Gale M., Kathleen J. Brown, and Ralph E. Reynolds. 2002. "Implications of Cognitive Resource Allocations for Comprehension Strategies Instruction." In *Comprehension Instruction: Researched-Based Best Practices*, ed. Cathy Collins Block and Michael Pressley, 62–76. New York: Guilford.

Smolkin, Laura B., and Carol A. Donovan. 2002. "'Oh Excellent, Excellent Question!': Developmental Differences and Comprehension Acquisition." In *Comprehension Instruction: Research-Based Best Practices*, ed. Cathy Collins Block and Michael Pressley, 140–57. New York: Guilford.

Snow, Catherine E., M. Susan Burns, and Peg Griffin, eds. 1998. *Preventing Reading Difficulties in Young Children*. Washington, DC: National Academy Press.

South Carolina State Department of Education. 2007. *South Carolina Academic Standards for English Language Arts*. Columbia, SC: SBE version, June 12, 2007.

Stahl, Steven. 1999. *Vocabulary Development*. Brookline, MA: Brookline.

Stahl, Steven A., and William E. Nagy. 2006. *Teaching Word Meanings*. Mahwah, NJ: Lawrence Erlbaum.

Taberski, Sharon. 2000. *On Solid Ground: Strategies for Teaching Reading, K–3*. Portsmouth, NH: Heinemann.

Taylor, Barbara M. 2002. "Highly Accomplished Primary Grade Teachers in Effective Schools." In *Teaching Reading: Effective Schools, Accomplished Teachers*, ed. Barbara M. Taylor and P. David Pearson, 279–88. Mahwah, NJ: Lawrence Erlbaum.

Taylor, Barbara M., P. David Pearson, Kathleen Clark, and Sharon Walpole. 1999. *Beating the Odds in Teaching All Children to Read*. CIERA Report #2-006. Ann Arbor, MI: CIERA.

———. 2002. "Effective Schools and Accomplished Teachers: Lessons About Primary-Grade Reading Instruction in Low-Income Schools." In *Teaching Reading: Effective Schools, Accomplished Teachers*, ed. Barbara M. Taylor and P. David Pearson, 3–72. Mahwah, NJ: Lawrence Erlbaum.

Taylor, Barbara, Debra S. Peterson, P. David Pearson, and Michael C. Rodriguez. 2002. "Looking Inside Classrooms: Reflecting on the 'How' as Well as the 'What' in Effective Reading Instruction." *The Reading Teacher* 56(3): 270–79.

Taylor, Barbara, Michael Pressley, and P. David Pearson. 2002. "Research-Supported Characteristics of Teachers and Schools That Promote Reading Achievement." In *Reading: Effective Schools, Accomplished Teachers*, ed. Barbara M. Taylor and P. David Pearson, 361–74. Mahwah, NJ: Lawrence Erlbaum.

Templeton, Shane, and Darrell Morris. 2002. "Spelling." In *Handbook of Reading Research*, vol. 3, ed. Michael L. Kamil, Peter B. Mosenthal, P. David Pearson, and Rebecca Barr, 525–44. Mahwah, NJ: Lawrence Erlbaum.

Towle, Wendy. 2000. "The Art of the Reading Workshop." *Educational Leadership* (September): 38–41.

Trabasso, Tom, and Edward Bouchard. 2002. "Teaching Readers How to Comprehend Text Strategically." In *Comprehension Instruction: Researched-Based Best Practices*, ed. Cathy Collins Block and Michael Pressley, 176–200. New York: Guilford.

Tracey, Diane H., and Lesley Mandel Morrow. 2002. "Preparing Young Learners for Successful Reading Comprehension: Laying the Foundation." In *Comprehension Instruction: Researched-Based Best Practices*, ed. Cathy Collins Block and Michael Pressley, 219–33. New York: Guilford.

Vygotsky, Lev S. 1980. *The Mind and Society: The Development of Higher Psychological Processes*. Cambridge, MA: Harvard University Press.

Weaver, Constance. 1994. *Reading Process and Practice: From Sociolinguistics to Whole Language*. Portsmouth, NH: Heinemann.

Wharton-McDonald, Ruth, Michael Pressley, and Jennifer M. Hampston. 1998. "Outstanding Literacy Instruction in First Grade: Teacher Practices and Student Achievement." *Elementary School Journal* 99: 101–28.

Williams, Joanna P. 2002. "Using the Theme Scheme to Improve Story Comprehension." In *Comprehension Instruction: Research-Based Best Practices*, ed. Cathy Block Collins and Michael Pressley, 126–39. New York: Guilford.

Index